I0571660

Young Changemakers

Make Your Mark

Volume 2

Kristi Maggio

Published by Maggio Multicultural Press

Maggio Multicultural Press books are available at special discounts for bulk purchases.

Book and cover design by Kristi Maggio
Edited and revised by Kristi Maggio
All co-authors wrote their own chapters.
Photography credit Sean Kanan's photo: Raquel Krelle Photography
First Edition

DEDICATION

This book is dedicated to the generations before us, whose courage, perseverance, and sacrifices laid the foundation for the opportunities that we all enjoy today. Coming from a family of immigrants, I honor the immense struggles they endured and the dreams they carried for a better future—for their children, their grandchildren, and those who follow; their legacy of resilience and hope should never be forgotten or taken for granted. May we continue to build on the paths they created and strive to leave our own for the generations to come.

This book is also dedicated to Ramy El-Batrawi. Your passing this year came far too soon, but your legacy and contributions will live on. Thank you for your inspiration, your wisdom, and the remarkable story you shared—a testament to the power of believing "you can really think and grow rich." We will continue to look at your journey as proof that these principles do work. I know you would have been a part of this book if you were still with us. You may be gone from this world, but you will never be forgotten.

Young Changemakers, Volume 2: Make Your Mark

Are you a young changemaker?

Want to be a part of the next volume of this series?

Visit young-changemakers.com & tell us your story!

Looking to become Future-Proof?

Join our *Future-Proof* course and start gaining the skills that will help you be successful no matter what you choose to do!

Visit maggiovirtualacademy.com

CONTENTS

Young Changemakers, Volume 2

ACKNOWLEDGMENTS

I would like to extend my deepest gratitude to all those who contributed to the creation of *Young Changemakers Volume 2*.

First and foremost, I want to thank the extraordinary young co-authors from around the world for sharing their inspiring stories. Your courage and dedication to making the world a better place are what this book is all about. Your efforts have made this book a reality, and for that, I am truly grateful.

I would also like to express my heartfelt appreciation to Sean Kanan, whose powerful foreword has added a deeply meaningful touch to this project.

A special thank you to our adult contributors—Lauren LaPointe, Queenie Donaldson, and Jona Lemmonds—who generously shared their wisdom in the "I Wish I Knew Then..." chapters.

I am grateful to the Maggio Multicultural Foundation for their support and commitment to creating educational opportunities for underserved youth around the world.

Lastly, to all the readers, mentors, and changemakers out there who invest their time in youth development, thank you for believing in the power of youth and for continuing to inspire future generations to make their mark on the world.

Together, we can create lasting change.
We are a T.E.A.M. because:
Together **E**veryone **A**chieves **M**ore

#COBRA

Sean Kanan's One Word

C - character

O - optimization

B - balance

R - respect

A – abundance

FOREWORD

by Sean Kanan

Emmy Award Winning Producer,
Emmy Nominated Actor,
Author

"Transform yourself, and you can transform the world." - *Sean Kanan*

Allow me to offer my congratulations to each of you reading this book and to those of you who have participated in creating its content. Whether you realize it or not, you are exceptional because you have done what most do not: take action. Too frequently, the vast majority of inhabitants on planet number three fail to act yet are often the first to cast judgment. You are making a difference in the world by engaging in solutions, not criticism; empowerment, not victimhood; and responsibility, not blame. Mahatma Gandhi said, "Be the change you wish to see in the world." Each of you embodies that change.

You are actively invested in your personal development, which not only expands your self-awareness but helps make the world a better place. More evolved humans make for a more evolved world for all of us. It's not unlike the Force in Star Wars. When we act in ways consistent with our highest selves, demonstrating empathy, love, and compassion, we give off a higher vibration, which in turn attracts more of the same from the universe and others. Engaging in actions that emit a low vibration, such as fear, jealousy, and anger, weakens the Force.

Like most of you, it's not difficult to find people, places, and things that I might've handled differently. Yet somehow, it has all brought me to the place I am now, which is pretty darn good. Often, what appears to be a mistake at the time or something unfortunate proves beneficial with the expansion of time. I can't help but think of the immortal lyrics of Frank

Sinatra from his iconic song, "My Way": "Regrets? I have a few, but then again, too few to mention." However, much of the information I now possess about both myself and the world around me would have come in pretty handy back in the day.

If I may offer one piece of advice to you and my younger self: "YOU ARE ENOUGH." The person that you want to be already exists within you. It's like the old Zen riddle, "How did the ship get into the bottle?" It was already there. Everything you need to live your most authentic and powerful life already lives within you. So often in life, we concern ourselves with becoming something else. I believe that much of life is about unbecoming. Work to shed the armor accumulated to protect us from the shame and criticism that we all encounter. Work to strip away the facade that hides our authentic self from both the world and ourselves.

The word "enough" also applies to the universe. In my book, *Way of the COBRA*, the word COBRA is an acronym formed from the words Character, Optimization, Balance, Respect, and Abundance. COBRAs are individuals living a life of authenticity and meaningful happiness while operating in a flow state. Sounds pretty next level? It is. It's also completely achievable for each of you. In fact, it's achievable for everyone because we live in a universe of abundance, not scarcity. There exists enough love, success, and happiness for all of us. Other people's success is not your failure. Other people's success does not diminish the possibility of you achieving success. This is the great truth of the universe. There's enough of everything for everyone. It's up to you to manifest it.

The first step to realizing this is believing it. COBRAs don't ruminate over the past or worry about the future (planning for the future is another thing altogether). COBRAs live in the present. If I had to choose one specific element that has the greatest potential impact on the trajectory of our lives and distill it down to one single word, that word would be character. Character is everything. Character is who you are at your core, your authentic self. True character means doing the right thing simply because it's the right thing to do—how you conduct yourself when there's no benefit to be had, simply because it's what should be done. Character, along with habits, defines your destiny. Guard it with your life. It can take a lifetime to build character, yet it can crumble in an instant. Some people use the words "character" and "reputation" interchangeably. They are very different. Reputation is what people say about us. It is almost entirely out of our control. Character is what we know to be true about ourselves—who we are at our core. Concentrate on your character, work hard, and be kind, and the universe will reward you with success and meaningful happiness. Now it's up to you. Go out and change the world.

INTRODUCTION

The path we walk today was built by the generations before us—those who worked hard, made sacrifices, and took risks to create the opportunities we now enjoy. Whether they realized it at the time or not, every step they took helped shape the world we live in. But their journey doesn't end with us. As we move forward, it's now our responsibility to continue paving the way, to leave behind a legacy that empowers and inspires those who will come after us. Every decision we make and every step we take adds to that story.

In *Young Changemakers Volume 2 Make Your Mark,* you'll meet remarkable young people from all over the world who are doing exactly that—using their voices to make a difference and proving that you don't have to wait until you're older to create change. These youth are choosing their own adventures, standing up for what they believe in, and leaving their mark on the world. They're not waiting for permission or the "right time." They're showing us that no matter your age, you can make an impact now. You have the power to write your own story, to choose the kind of world you want to live in and help build it for future generations.

Here's something we often forget: choosing your own path doesn't mean ignoring the past. There is so much we can learn from those who came before us. Their stories—both the successes and the failures—are filled with lessons that can help guide us. So, while it's important to forge ahead and create something new, it's just as important to listen, to learn, and to be open to the advice and experiences others share with us. You never know when something someone says or does might spark a new idea or give you the insight you need to overcome a challenge.

However, while it's crucial to listen to the wisdom of others, we must also remember that no one else knows your journey the way you do. Sometimes, people may advise caution or suggest you play it safe, not because they doubt your abilities, but because they couldn't achieve something themselves. Their limitations don't have to be yours. Their doubts don't define your potential. You have to trust yourself, your vision, and your ability to navigate your own path. Yes, mistakes will happen, but mistakes aren't failures—they're opportunities to grow, to learn, and to build character. The only real failure is not trying because you were too afraid of the unknown.

Fear can be a powerful force. It often comes from not knowing what lies ahead, from the endless "what ifs" that we let take over our thoughts. But here's the thing: fear only has power if you let it stop you from moving forward. You don't have to have all the answers right away, and you don't need to know every step of the journey to start. What matters is that you take action, even when it's scary, even when the path is unclear. Because every time you step forward into the unknown, you're not just moving closer to your goals—you're also paving the way for others who will follow in your footsteps.

In this book, you will see how these young changemakers have faced their fears, embraced their mistakes, and used their voices to create change. They've chosen their adventures, made their mark, and are now lighting the way for others. Their stories will remind you that success doesn't come from following someone else's path—it comes from having the courage to create your own.

You have a voice, and it matters. No matter how young or old you are, your ideas, your dreams, and your actions can make a difference. So take the lessons of the past, combine them with your vision for the future, and go out and create something incredible. Don't be afraid to take risks, to make mistakes, and to stand up for what you believe in. Remember, the mark you leave today will inspire the generations who come after you, just as those before you have inspired you. This is your time to make your mark, to choose your adventure, and to lead the way for others.

CHAPTER 1

#ENERGY
Sachin's One Word

E - energize the room

N - never give up

E - engage your mind 24/7

R - revolutionize

G - gratitude

Y - your network is your net worth

Young Changemakers, Volume 2: Make Your Mark

GO FOR IT: UNLEASH YOUR GAME-CHANGING ENERGY

by Sachin Syal

Award-Winning Entrepreneur & Podcaster
Host of "The O'ChakDe Show"
Co-Founder & CEO of 3Doshas

"If you want to be successful in life, utilize the power of ask."
- *Sachin Syal*

From a young age, I've always felt a calling to inspire others, particularly young people, to chase their dreams and make them a reality. I realized that this was my purpose, my mission, and therefore, I work to inspire millions of young people to "go for it" in life and chase their true dreams. I'm bringing this mission to life through my podcast, The O'ChakDe Show, on YouTube. We are Silicon Valley's first ever revenue-generating business and self-improvement podcast for teens, hosted by a teen (me!). "O'ChakDe" is a Punjabi word and it means "Go For It!" On the show, I interview remarkable and influential entrepreneurs, executives, investors, leaders, and inspiring individuals from all walks of life so we can learn from their stories and level up ourselves. I've had the honor to have billionaires like Tim Draper and Naveen Jain appear on my show. Other top guests include industry legends such as Brad Smith, Mark Suster, Guy Kawasaki, Nirav Tolia, Neil Patel, Anthony Pompliano, David Meltzer, Evan Carmichael, Bracken Darrell, Anthony Di Iorio, Joe De Sena, Patty McCord, Brian Scudamore, Monty Moran, Mauro Porcini, Beto Guajardo, and many more influential people. I've also interviewed former professional athletes from the NBA and NFL turned entrepreneurs and investors. I currently have 175,000+ international views on my channel. I've also worked with many paid company sponsors and have made thousands of dollars through The O'ChakDe Show, all through lots of hustling and networking. These companies pay me to promote their product or service on my episodes. My goal in the future is to transform The O'ChakDe Show into a huge media empire and online community. I want teens to know that age is just a number and that finding a purpose or passion in life is truly life changing. You will have something to always look forward to and be excited about and this plays a crucial role in your well-being and confidence levels. My slogan is "Go For It" and I chose that because I'm a big believer in the phrase: stop thinking, start doing. I am also contributing to the world by coaching people on my lifestyle and wellness coaching platform 3Doshas.com, where I'm the Co-Founder & CEO. We are transforming lives through 3Doshas energies from Yoga & Ayurveda with hundreds of international active users.

The world of social media is a vast one, and one that I think is a double-edged sword. Personally, I love social media as it's helped me with personal branding and the growth of my podcast and company. Social media can be a great place to connect with new people and share your goals with an audience. You can also reach out to people you look up to for mentorship and cold call people you want to collaborate with. If you're a content creator, consistently posting content can help you gain more followers and monetize your passion. Social media becomes dangerous when you become addicted to it. If you're always scrolling through TikTok or Instagram aimlessly for hours, that's a problem, because it can lead to mental and physical health problems. It's just temporary dopamine and then you'll keep looking for more. The way I look at it is that you can either be a creator or a consumer. I will always choose to be a creator, and I've learned that creators will always be creators. Social media is a great invention, and I think more people need to become open-minded about the benefits but also cautious of the drawbacks.

Growing up I was always interested in sales and marketing. In elementary and middle school, I used to sell candy, stickers, and toys to other kids at school for profit, making hundreds of dollars as a pre-teen. I found my natural knack for entrepreneurship at a very young age and wanted to take it to the next level, so I started an eBay store. I started selling old things around my house that weren't being used anymore. Unfortunately, my first sale didn't go so well. I still remember how happy I was when I saw I got a buyer on my listing for an old phone. I ran to my parents and showed them the notification from eBay. However, it was not as happy of a story as I had wanted it to be. Unfortunately, I got scammed by this buyer and the money disappeared on PayPal. This was a tough time for me because despite trying my best and explaining the situation to customer service, I had lost the money. During this time, I could have easily given up and quit with the mindset of I'm too young and inexperienced to be an eBay reseller, but I didn't! I genuinely think if I gave up there and then, I wouldn't be writing this book. From that day on, I turned my failure into a lesson and never got scammed again.

Through consistently and persistently selling products on eBay, I generated over 5 figures in sales at 13 years old during the pandemic. I learned that by not giving up I created a life for myself as an entrepreneur and podcaster. From making the right choice of not giving up years ago, I found a purpose in my life. I live and breathe entrepreneurship, advertising, podcasting, personal branding, networking, and these things keep me up at night and wake me up in the morning excited to start a new day. Some of my biggest accomplishments as a teen are that I've been featured on Bloomberg TV which is national television and I'm the recipient of the JA (Junior Achievement) Worldwide Impact Award on 2 Minute Drill; I've been featured in a Freethink, by Stand Together, professional documentary and was filmed on set. I'm a TEDx Speaker, and I've been interviewed on air on the biggest South Asian radio station in the US. If I simply quit and had a negative fixed mindset about my failure back then, I wouldn't have achieved everything I've done in my life so far. One success will lead to another, and then it's a ripple effect. You need to trust the process. I'm very grateful that I didn't give up, and I never plan to.

My vision is to help millions of people level up through The O'ChakDe Show and 3Doshas. I want to create an in-person studio for my podcast in the Bay Area and run it like a talk show. I want to grow my coaching platform and gain many more users. I want to teach and show the world the benefits of Yoga & Ayurveda for success in all aspects of life.

My one word is Energy. To me, it means always striving to energize the room, never giving up, and engaging my mind 24/7. It's about revolutionizing the way I approach challenges, embracing gratitude in all aspects of life, and recognizing that your network is truly your net worth. This word encapsulates the drive, persistence, and connection I bring to everything I do.

If you're reading this, please keep going. Life is like a rocket ship, there are always going to be ups and downs, just make sure you don't stop rising! And I will come to an end and leave you with these quotes. They inspired me, and I hope they will inspire you as well:

"Happiness comes from enjoying the consistent and persistent pursuit of your potential." - David Meltzer

"Life needs to be more than just solving problems every day. You need to wake up and be excited about the future." - Elon Musk

Chapter 2

12.29.18 05.28.19 08.17.21 04.09.22

08.06.22 04.27.23 06.16.23 06.28.23

07.12.23 04.06.24 05.03.24 08.06.24

journey.

#JOURNEY
Khushi's One Word

J – jump out of your comfort zone & into new passions

O – orient yourself with your goals, purpose, and discipline

U – unapologetically stay true to who you are

R – reflect on your progress often

N – network actively to inspire and be inspired

E – embrace the failures & learning opportunities just as much as the successes

Y – yearn for moments, not just the destination – you only get this journey once!

JOURNEY > DESTINATION: MY MOMENTS OF INNOVATION, GROWTH & IMPACT

By Khushi Shah

Tech Innovator, Entrepreneur, Mentor

"Never say no to an adventure, especially if it is outside of your comfort zone... you never know which one might change your life." – Khushi Shah

Hi there! I'm Khushi Shah, a 19-year-old dynamo on a mission to redefine the world through innovation and inspiration. As the Founder & CEO of Drizzl (formerly E-Code) currently navigating my way through Northeastern University, I wear many hats—a tech innovator, trailblazing entrepreneur, and global youth mentor.

An avid *Shark Tank* viewer since the age of 10, my mission has always been crystal clear: contribute to the world on the fronts of entrepreneurship and social impact. However, it wasn't until a family trip in middle school that I truly understood the urgency of this mission. Seeing people struggle without key resources, like water, was eye-opening. I knew I wanted to make a difference and had my "aha" moment when I saw someone back home with their sprinklers on in the rain.

That same year, I developed the first prototype of my proprietary smart irrigation system, Drizzl, for my school's science fair. What started as a simple research project quickly gained traction, leading me to discover its potential as a real product. Numerous prototypes and pitch competitions/accelerators later, I can proudly say Drizzl began making a real impact and has been recognized by major organizations including Google, NASA, the US Navy, and my hometown has honored me by proclaiming a day in my name

- all by the time I was 17.

But life is all about the unexpected, right? Growing up in, and navigating, 3 countries and 14 schools has certainly yielded a series of pivotal moments in my life. Most recently, graduating high school a year early and taking a gap year in place of my senior year turned out to be the most off-script, but rewarding decision of my journey. My experience was all about diving headfirst into my entrepreneurial ventures, and the outcomes surpassed my wildest expectations. Now, I'm studying abroad in London, balancing academics, business expansion, and even competed in a reality TV show for eco-entrepreneurs—a chapter I had always dreamed of, and going better than I could have ever imagined.

However, my vision goes beyond personal success. I dream of a future where youth globally, irrespective of gender or background, have opportunities to turn their ideas into reality. As an Indian American female armed with unique skills from my global upbringing, I strive to leave the world more inclusive and empowered. I'm a global youth mentor, reaching over 3000 students worldwide through my "Build-A-Business Workshop". I also use my platform to amplify voices for causes close to my heart. Through these educational initiatives and diverse perspectives, I aim to create an environment where young individuals can drive change in their own lives, and others', beyond just the duration of the workshop.

From all my adventures, my one word is JOURNEY—a concept we often overlook in our pursuit of destinations. Journeying means jumping out of your comfort zone and into new passions, orienting yourself with goals, purpose, and discipline, and unapologetically staying true to who you are. It's about reflecting on your progress often, actively networking to inspire and be inspired, and embracing failures as much as successes, recognizing that rejection is simply redirection. Above all, it's about yearning for the moments, not just the destination, because you only get this journey once!

Remember, "Never say no to an adventure, especially if it is outside of your comfort zone...you never know which one might change your life." This is an ideology that I apply to all aspects of my life, whether I am working on Drizzl, avidly traveling the world, or just spending quality time with my people. I'm here, writing my chapter of inspiration, making a mark on the world, and confidently believe that every young person has the potential to do the same.

CHAPTER 3

#RESILIENCE
Tanuj's One Word

R - rise up every time you fall

E - ever onward

S - stars don't shine without darkness

I - impossibility is a myth

L - leave a legacy

I - in the depth of winter, there is within you an invincible summer! Find that.

E - enjoy the process

N - 'now' is the right time to start doing anything, don't wait, act!

C - challenge yourself every day to perform better than your previous self

E - end is the new beginning, don't lose hope.

FAIL AGAIN, FAIL HARDER

by Tanuj Samaddar, FRSA

Artist, Youth Advocate

"Aim for the moon, even if you miss, you'll land on the stars."
- Norman Vincent Peale

My mission isn't singular; it's a colorful mix of different ideas and passions all coming together. I believe in creating a generation based on moral strength, character, willpower, and hard work. Through my work and ideas, I endeavor to motivate my peers to pursue excellence in whatever they do rather than fixating their minds on the consequences of their actions.

As an artist, I see the world as a canvas overflowing with untold stories. From the furrowed brow of a classmate grappling with a concept to the quiet strength of a community leader, these narratives yearn to be captured. Through my artworks, I bring various social issues of current significance to the forefront, attracting public attention and capturing their imagination. My work bridges the gap between artistic expression and social activism, giving voice to critical issues through visual narratives that resonate across cultural boundaries. I believe I am not just creating art, but I am wielding creativity as a powerful tool for social change and global awareness.

As a Councilor in the Global Youth Advisory Council Zimbabwe, I'm at the forefront of addressing one of the most pressing issues of our time: youth mental health. I believe my focus on this area is crucial, as mental health challenges among young people have been escalating globally, exacerbated by factors such as social media pressure, academic stress, and societal expectations. By spearheading campaigns and creating short films, I'm not only raising awareness but also destigmatizing mental health issues, encouraging open dialogue, and providing accessible information to those who need it most. My debut short video series titled *Metamorphosis*, which has now been listed on IMDb, focuses on the complexities of interpersonal relationships and the need for introspection among youths.

My experience as a peer counselor during my school days laid the foundation for my current focus on mental health issues. This early exposure to the challenges faced by my peers likely informed my understanding of youth mental health, giving me invaluable insights that now shape my advocacy work. It demonstrates a long-standing commitment to supporting others, a trait that undoubtedly contributes to the authenticity and effectiveness of my current initiatives.

Recently, I've joined Human Nature Projects Ontario as a Summer Fellow and participated in different environmental workshops and global networking opportunities. I'll be tasked with preparing a report on the effect of the climate crisis on the indigenous communities of Canada.

Art has considerable potential in peacebuilding, not only in the conflict resolution field but also in post-conflict reconciliation. Defying all linguistic boundaries, it is considered a universal language and therefore an ideal resource to understand the perspectives of others, particularly their perspective on a given conflict. Art can also directly nurture a peace process by providing a voice to marginalized or oppressed groups while enhancing the relevance and legitimacy of the process itself. The use of art can be strategic, particularly during negotiations and mediation processes when verbal communication reaches its limits. Art is a powerful instrument for collective reconciliation between communities, and it can equally be useful for individuals to overcome any trauma linked to conflict.

Through my involvement with organizations like Kiran Foundation (India), International Women's Peace Group (South Korea), and the World Organization for Sustainability and Leadership, I want to paint a picture of holistic social change at the grassroots level, transcending cultural boundaries and embodying the Indian motto 'Vasudhaiva Kutumbakam,' which means 'The World is my Family.'

My perspective on social media reflects duality, considering the mixed effects it has on the minds of people. According to me, social media is a double-edged sword; its utility is starkly juxtaposed against the devastating effects it has on today's youth. Its genesis as a mode to bring people together through various online platforms seems rather ironic considering the staggering repercussions portraying the decay of interpersonal relationships and lack of open communication among people, most of which could be attributed to the increasing addiction to social media. While most of us can stay in touch with our friends and family through platforms like Facebook and Instagram, traditional familial bonds are falling apart ironically because of the existence of these platforms.

Social media has had mixed effects on my life. During the pandemic period, social media greatly helped me to find and participate in different national and international level competitions. I was exposed to newer opportunities and people through platforms like Instagram and Facebook in particular. Opportunities to participate in different conferences and network with like-minded individuals did widen my scope and reach not only in the field of fine arts but in other allied fields. But I must admit, during those days I did become addicted to these platforms, and my screen time spiked up.

I believe that we should have a balanced approach whenever it comes to using social media platforms. Extensive usage of these platforms could be counterproductive, but when utilized in a proper manner, they help in forging new connections, acquiring new skills, gaining more exposure, and learning new things.

There have been many such red-letter moments in my life that acted as turning points. I cannot diminish the importance of international recognitions like the Kentucky Colonel Commissionship, Nomination for the International Children's Peace Prize, Fellowship of the Royal Society of Arts, or even the U.S. President's Education Award or any other international award I clinched in the many art competitions I had participated in. But the Pradhan Mantri Rashtriya Bal Puraskar 2021 (THE PRESIDENT'S AWARD) was one such recognition that I will hold dear to my heart. It was one such pivotal time in my life when I had the rare opportunity to meet the Prime Minister of India among many other dignitaries. I held quite an insightful conversation with him and was accompanied by my parents and the Hon. District Magistrate.

Apart from that, my selection to be a part of the Clippers Child Council of India helped me get connected to a bright network of achievers nationwide and beyond. Another important event was my selection as a Councilor in the prestigious Global Youth Advisory Council of Art of Health Zimbabwe, London School of Hygiene and Tropical Medicine. Being a council member, I am able to spearhead many youth-related initiatives in my region. Leading awareness campaigns and conferences and having organizational support has provided my community service and commitment to social change with proper orientation. In 2022, I was also awarded the coveted GLOBAL KIDS ACHIEVERS AWARD for my excellence in the field of Fine Arts and Social Welfare. It was another dream come true moment for me, but there is also a story behind these accolades of persistence and strength.

My journey has resilience as its pulse – a path that began at two with a paintbrush in my hands. I learned early in life that resilience is a powerful agent of change rather than just an instrument for survival. Growing up in a low-income family, societal biases and doubts could have easily stifled my dreams. Each stroke of my brush became a testament to resilience, channeling personal struggles into powerful artistic expressions that resonated globally. It cut across challenges that were never very convenient. I encountered so many hurdles – lack of funds, social norms, and the general vices of pursuing art when all around you, people doubt your abilities and choices. However, each of them turned into growing and proving that it was possible to open the world and make people listen to my voice regardless of being disabled.

So for me, resilience is much more than simply the ability to keep going as many other authors have defined this term. It is not a plan—a concrete set of strategies to avoid misfortune and overcome them if met. It increased my drive to address sustainability challenges through art and made me want to be more active in creating change among people. Each painting was a conflict in which optimism stood up against skepticism, and where enthusiasm for one's work stood up against obstacles. Moreover, resilience permeated every facet of my life. It wasn't just about artistic pursuits but also about academic excellence. Now when I look back, I find that there has always been a twilight existence of rebellion within me. Through resilience, I sought out and secured state and national-level scholarships, proving my mettle and reinforcing the importance of self-reliance in achieving one's goals.

My artistic journey has been marked with numerous struggles, making this journey worth embarking on. The town I belong to is a beautiful one nestled in the scenic beauty of the state of Assam, but it equally faces the problem of resource scarcity whenever it comes to skill acquisition. Gaining expertise in this field was a personal endeavor with bare minimum resources. It often becomes difficult to compete with artists having relatively more resources when one knows that one possesses the equivalent skill in this field.

Added to this crisis was societal bias, which is very well predictable as I hail from a low-income group, and I was no other exception. At times, I was segregated from peer groups based on my financial status. But for me, competence and capability are all that matter, and I'm a self-fulfilled and self-reliant individual and didn't let the naysayers get the better of my wits. During those times, all I could do was fine-tune my skills with or without proper guidance. I started using online resources to learn various techniques and brushstrokes, although it was quite a time-taking and cumbersome process, it was definitely worth the effort. My family, especially my mother, became my constant source of motivation. I would advise my readers to anchor their faith in their family whenever things get harder for them - there's no greater strength than that.

Now whenever I become emotionally or mentally overwhelmed, I practice mindfulness and self-introspection. It's imperative that we cultivate a solution-oriented mindset rather than focusing on the problems or troubles that bother us. I review my scheme of actions and try to find any probable loopholes, then I work on undoing the issue if it's possible at my end. If not, I focus on making the remaining course of the task as error-free as possible. It's important that we recognize the inner strength and get motivated by realizing how far we have trodden the path of life, gathering important bittersweet experiences during the ever-ongoing journey. And each of these experiences makes us who we are today. To those who are reading this, whenever you make a choice, think about how the outcome would impact the generations yet to come. If we focus on what legacy we would be leaving behind, I believe all of us would be able to make better choices in our lives. And this very idea should motivate us to keep doing productive work for our family, community, and the nation.

I believe the answers to the aforementioned questions encompass the major aspects of the suggestions I would have given to my readers. But I would like to reiterate some of the advice:

FAMILY: Stay close to your family, that helps you stay connected to your roots. Build a family based on moral values strengthened by virtues like spirituality, respect for elders among others. Remember, FAMILY comes first. In most cases, your family will always stand by you under all and any circumstances, and at times they would need you and your leadership.

LEGACY: Work so hard that you leave behind a legacy for your next generations to feel proud of. Ensure that they become capable enough to become responsible trustees of your legacy and carry that forward.

FAILURE: Remember you are preparing for the WAR called life. The victory in this WAR would solely be determined by the experiences you've gained by accumulating many failures in different BATTLES of your life. These failures will prepare you for the WAR. This very advice resonates with the CHAPTER TITLE: FAIL AGAIN, FAIL HARDER.

LOSING PEOPLE: In life, you'll lose people. They might be those who are really close to you. People, with whom you've seen millions of dreams together. These episodes set your life for the better or worse. Make sure that it comes as a blessing and transforms you for your own good. These people are unworthy of your time and effort. God has removed them from your life so that you could have the opportunity to meet better people in your life. People who actually matter. People who deserve you. Know your worth and don't look back. REMEMBER GOD IS PROTECTING YOU.

FRIENDS: You'll befriend many people in this short journey

called life. But few of them will be your closest ones. Make good choices when it comes to selecting people you would be relying upon in your life; these people will be your friends. Keep them close and never let the rust of time corrode the beautiful brotherhood you will be developing/have developed with your close friends.

WORK: Work is important, but you are more important. While trying to maintain your professional life, don't ignore your personal and emotional well-being.

GRADES MATTER: Don't play on extremities, don't stress yourself beyond a certain limit just for the sake of grades but try to maintain a decent academic track record. Trust me, it helps a lot.

DO WHAT YOU LOVE: Do what gives you unending bliss. Break the rules, push your boundaries, and explore new ideas. You've got this one life, enjoy every aspect of it. Make sure you have memorable stories from your life to tell the generations that are yet to come. Your stories shall ignite a different type of spark in their hearts.

BE REMEMBERED FOR GOOD!

There are many quotes I live by, and a few of them are:

"Antah Asti Prarambha" - this is a SANSKRIT phrase meaning: End is the new beginning and signifies infinity. It says don't lose hope if you've lost something, or if something has ended, there will always be a new start, a new beginning, and a new chapter to every conclusion.

"Aim for the moon, even if you miss, you'll land on the stars."
- Norman Vincent Peale

"I WISH I KNEW THEN..."

By Queenie Donaldson

Founder and CEO Queens Entertainment Group, Inc., Entrepreneur, Entertainment consultant, Speaker

Looking back, the most significant lesson I've learned is the importance of personal growth and trusting the inner voice that has always been there to guide me. When I was younger, I often sought answers from the world around me, thinking I needed the advice and approval of others to find my way. I wish I had known then what I know now: that my inner voice—God's quiet whisper—was all I ever truly needed to navigate life's challenges.

As I've grown older, I've realized that my intuition, that deep sense of knowing, has been my most reliable guide. When I listen to it, when I have the courage to trust it, things fall into place in ways that are almost miraculous. But when I ignored it—whether out of fear, doubt, or the influence of others—I struggled.

I wish I had the strength to keep going, no matter what, when I was younger. Now, I understand that strength and courage aren't just about pushing through the hard times but also about trusting that I'm on the right path, even when the way forward seems unclear. If I had that knowledge and inner resolve earlier, I know I would have embraced more opportunities and faced fewer setbacks.

In my entrepreneurial journey, this has proven especially true. But life in general teaches us this: as we grow and evolve, we must continue to listen to our inner voice, adjusting our course when necessary, and having the courage to follow it even when it's difficult.

I've also learned that personal growth requires continually building and renewing the village of people around us. Some will come and go, and we must adjust when we lose those who were once integral parts of our lives. This has been one of the most challenging aspects of my journey—adapting to the loss of those who were part of my village and finding the courage to build new circles when needed.

Now, I understand the importance of seeking help for mental fitness at every stage of life. Taking care of our emotional and mental well-being is as vital as any other part of our journey. It gives us the strength to keep going and the clarity to continue following our inner voice, regardless of the obstacles in our path.

If I could go back and give my younger self advice, I would tell her to trust in her strength and courage. I would tell her that everything she needs is already inside of her, and that if she just listens to that voice and continues moving forward, everything will work out. I would remind her that personal growth is ongoing, and the ability to adjust and keep building the right village is just as important as any goal she sets her mind to.

To the next generation......Have faith in your own voice. Trust that deep sense of knowing within you—it will guide you through the most difficult moments. Be courageous, even when the path seems unclear, and remember that setbacks are often just setups for something greater. Continue to build and nurture your village, and don't be afraid to adjust your circle as you grow. Take care of your mind, heart, and spirit, because your mental fitness will carry you further than you can imagine. Most importantly, keep going no matter what. You are stronger and braver than you realize, and everything you need to succeed is already within you.

CHAPTER 4

#CONNECT
Biah's One Word

C - cherish the bonds you have made with people

O - open up your mind to different ideas and perspectives

N - nothing is more fulfilling than giving back to the world

N - never think you're on your own; reach out to your loved ones when you feel hopeless

E - everything will turn out for the better if you embrace change positively

C - create your own opportunities if you have to

T - try to be your most authentic self

CONNECTING THROUGH COMPASSION

by Biah Umer Khan

Connector, Journalist, Advocate for Social Justice,
Community Volunteer, President of Irteqaa

"Don't borrow grief from the future." - Unkown

Hello readers! To begin this chapter, let me introduce myself. I'm Biah Umer Khan, an A-level student from Lahore, Pakistan. I'm passionate about journalism and community service, and I've been lucky enough to combine these interests through my NGO, Irteqaa. When I'm not working on my projects, you can usually find me reading, writing, or—though I hate to admit it—scrolling through Instagram reels.

From a young age, I've been driven by a mission to create safe spaces and communities where people are tolerant and open to different ways of thinking. I believe that journalism is a powerful tool to promote social justice, which is why I've poured so much of my energy into Irteqaa. By teaching teenagers the value of honest reporting and a moral responsibility to uphold the truth, I hope to encourage my generation to promote and advocate for social justice. During my year-long term as President of Irteqaa, we've grown to 4.3k followers and have organized internships in media and journalism for nearly a hundred students from across Pakistan.

One project particularly close to my heart is Irteqaa's Child Education Task Force, which I co-founded in August 2023. This initiative aims to raise funds for the education of underprivileged children and connect them with potential sponsors. Educational opportunities are something that matter a great deal to me; I have always loved school. Even before the school year would start, I would read through all my textbooks and novels that were part of the curriculum for that year. During school days, the first thing I would do when I got home was pull out my notebooks and get done with my homework immediately. For all my life, I have genuinely enjoyed the process of learning. So, knowing that many children in my country have been deprived of such wonderful educational experiences has made me determined to tackle illiteracy in my community.

I am a very sensitive person by nature; I get easily upset by anyone else's suffering and this helps me keep myself connected to my community without shutting myself in a secure bubble. This sensitivity often translates into a strong desire for achieving justice. Cruelty and oppression of the truth always makes me feel frustrated, and I try to channel these emotions into honest journalism at Irteqaa. It is always my priority to ensure my team confronts their internal biases and discards one-sided reporting.

Social media has played a big role in Irteqaa's success. Irteqaa operates completely on social media platforms, and I can't deny how this has enabled us to have widespread impact. Our vision of being able to report on neglected issues through student journalism is only fulfilled because of the reach we get on our main page. Lots of young people, including myself, get most of their news from social media. So, what we try to do at Irteqaa is compile information from multiple credible sources and present a holistic overview of an issue from both sides.

From a marketing aspect, social media is also a great tool to get traction and raise funds for different causes. For instance, we were able to advertise a Futsal Fundraiser in my city for high school teams. Many local teams have created their own social media pages so it is easier to reach them directly on that platform and motivate them to participate. We managed to raise more than Rs. 63000, which all went towards funding a former child laborer's education.

However, while all these advantages exist, I personally have a problem with the tendency to end up doom scrolling on social media. Sometimes I cannot regulate my usage and end up seeing overwhelming news without any breaks; this just puts me in a static position where I feel unable to function. When we get too much news too quickly, instead of feeling well-informed we end up feeling numb or desensitized.

Throughout my journey, I've faced my share of challenges, but I've learned to stay motivated by focusing on what truly matters to me—creating positive change in my community. I believe success isn't just about happiness; it's synonymous to a sense of fulfillment. True success comes when you find a way to align your passions, dreams, and skills in a way that gives back to the world. There's nothing more peaceful or satisfying than doing something that makes a difference in someone else's life.

Looking ahead, I want to continue working on my passions in a way that positively impacts society. No matter what career path I choose, I know that community service will always be a part of my life. My advice to other young people who want to make a difference is simple: take action. It's easy to sit back and plan how you would solve a problem, but what really matters is getting out there and doing something about it. Start small: volunteer, participate in school drives, and make connections with people who share your interests. Collaboration is key to creating a bigger impact, so don't be afraid to step out of your comfort zone and find others who are willing to help.

For me, the word that defines everything I do, my one word is "Connect." Whether it's connecting with myself, others, or my community, it's the most important thing in my life. I love my own space and spending time with my own thoughts, trying to get in touch with my true self. I also deeply care about the bonds and relationships I form with other people; there is nothing I feel more grateful for than my loved ones. Lastly, connecting with my community is important to me because I firmly believe we all have a responsibility to connect with our communities and do good in the world.

There are a few quotes that I live by, but one that stands out is, "Don't borrow grief from the future." I have a tendency to stress about things that are out of my control, but this quote reminds me to stay grounded and appreciate the present moment. It's a lesson I try to carry with me every day as I navigate my journey of connecting with the world and making a difference.

CHAPTER 5

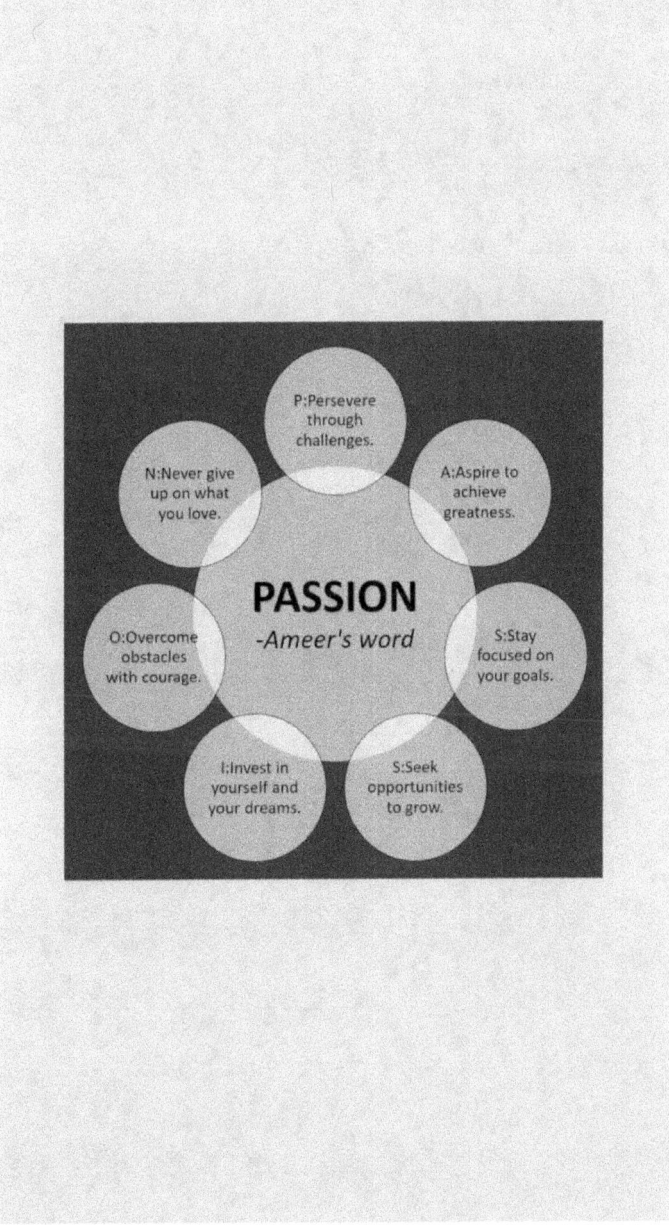

#PASSION
Ameer's One Word

P - persevere through challenges.

A - aspire to achieve greatness.

S - stay focused on your goals.

S - seek opportunities to grow.

I - invest in yourself and your dreams.

O - overcome obstacles with courage.

N - never give up on what you love.

THE JOURNEY OF A YOUNG INNOVATOR

by Ameer El-Kurd

Motivated Tech Maker, Creator and Inventor of Pleasidea

"If something bad happens, don't sit in a corner expecting it to be fixed, go on an adventure to fix it. Because time doesn't fix everything."
- Ameer El-Kurd

I am Ameer El-Kurd, a young tech maker, creator, and the inventor of Pleasidea. My mission is simple: to help people all over the world. I do this in my own unique way—by creating technology that supports people both mentally and physically. Whether it's developing AI that can talk to someone who needs a listening ear or designing robots that can do heavy labor like extinguishing fires or cleaning up our beaches, my goal is always the same—to make life better for others.

Social media has been a big part of my journey, and I've learned to see it as an environment all on its own. You can choose how you want to use it. Some people get caught up in the addictive, fabricated content that social media can offer, but for me, it's been a tool for growth. I've watched countless motivational videos and learned about topics I didn't fully understand in school. LinkedIn, in particular, has been a game-changer. It's allowed me to connect with amazing people who share the same mindset and goals as I do, and through these connections, I've been able to complete many of the projects I've worked on over the years. Right now, I'm focused on expanding my network even further and meeting new people who can help me achieve my goals.

One of the most pivotal moments in my life happened during the creation of my first robot. It was for the final week of a course I was taking, and honestly, it was one of the most stressful experiences I've ever had. I always start my projects with a clear vision, and this one was no different. I wanted to create a firefighter robot that could be controlled wirelessly using WiFi and charged with solar panels to make it eco-friendly. However, as I dove into the project, I quickly realized I was in over my head. The parts failed on me, the solar panels wouldn't charge, and time was slipping away.

I was faced with a tough decision: either give up and submit an incomplete project or find a new way to achieve my goal. The stress was intense. I thought about it constantly, becoming more and more nervous as the days passed. Then, one day, I decided to take a break. I filled up the bath and just relaxed for a bit, and that's when it hit me. I remembered an idea from an older course I had taken at the same academy. It was the perfect solution. I jumped out of the bath and started working on it immediately. And it worked! The project came together just in time, and I ended up securing the gold medal, which is how the academy rewards and rates students. It was one of the happiest moments of my life, knowing that all my hard work and dedication paid off in the end.

Looking ahead, I see the future as a place for positive change. People all over the world are seeking better opportunities to achieve their dreams, and I'm no different. I want to continue helping people by creating projects and expanding my network. Meeting new people and getting better at what I do are priorities for me, and I don't think my main objective—helping people—is going to change. I'm committed to improving and creating opportunities not just for myself, but for others as well.

If I had to sum up what drives me in one word, it would be passion. Passion is my one word. To me, it is a mix of love, appreciation, and even a little bit of anger. It's a feeling like no other, that desire to be seen, to be acknowledged for what you can do. Passion makes you stronger and more efficient in your work, and it's what keeps me going every day.

I live by two quotes that guide me through life. The first is from Martin Luther King Jr., something I've learned over time: "No matter what, you will always be you." It's a reminder to stay true to myself. The second is something I've come up with on my own: "If something bad happens, don't sit in a corner expecting it to be fixed. Go on an adventure to fix it. Because time doesn't fix everything." This quote speaks to my belief that action is always better than inaction. If you want something to change, you have to be the one to make it happen.

My journey is just beginning, but I'm excited about what the future holds. I'm determined to keep pushing the boundaries of what's possible and to continue making a difference in the world, one project at a time.

CHAPTER 6

#COMPASSION
Sarah's One Word

C - caring; showing concern for others

O - open-minded; acceptance towards others

M - mindfulness; awareness of others' needs, and acting accordingly

P - patience; understanding in challenging situations

A - authenticity; sincerity with others

S - supporting; encouraging of others

S - self-achievement; valuing personal goals and growth

I - integrity; continuing efforts for trustworthiness in relationships

O - optimistic; a consistent positive attitude

N - nurturing; adopting development, growth, and achievement in others and oneself

COMPASSION IN ACTION: RAISING AWARENESS THROUGH CONNECTION

by Sarah Sami

Visual Communicator, Health Advocate,
Advocate for Underrepresented Populations

"It is not the word that is important, it is the idea and ambition behind it."
- Emma Watson

Hello! My name is Sarah Sami, and I am a grade 10 student from Multan, Pakistan. With a strong academic background in Digital Design, I have developed a passion for digital marketing, design, and visual communication. Beyond academics, I am deeply involved in community and service projects, where I've honed my skills in communication, teamwork, and creative expression. Whether it's through writing, reading, or photography, I find joy in exploring and highlighting the stories that often go unnoticed.

My mission is to raise awareness about underrepresented health issues in Pakistan while simultaneously celebrating the rich diversity of cultures around the world. Through my work, I aim to inspire empathy, promote deeper understanding, and spark meaningful action, ultimately making a lasting impact in my community and beyond. By shedding light on these crucial health concerns, I hope to bring attention to the challenges faced by those who often go unheard. In addition to this, I am passionate about highlighting the rich backgrounds of certain cultures and areas, focusing on the unique traditions and characteristics that these places are known for. By increasing visibility and knowledge about such wonderful and diverse regions, I aspire to inspire action, promote empathy, and celebrate the beauty of diversity. It is through this dual focus—on both health issues and cultural appreciation—that I believe we can build a more inclusive, understanding, and compassionate world.

I have a gift, and that gift is my unique innate ability to deeply resonate with people and their stories. This ability allows me to connect on a profound level with individuals from all walks of life, understanding their experiences and emotions in a way that goes beyond the surface. I have a sharp eye for identifying overlooked issues, those that often go unnoticed by others, and a passion for giving a platform to the unheard voices, especially through the writing skills that I possess. Through my writing, I strive to bring these stories to the forefront, ensuring that they receive the attention they deserve. I am able to explore and celebrate diverse perspectives, finding the beauty and value in the differences that make each person and community unique. My goal is to provide great understanding and appreciation for people and communities, creating a more connected and empathetic world where every voice is heard and valued.

While the world has different views on social media, it is a crucial part of my mission and what I aim to achieve. Social media provides a platform to connect with people from all walks of life. It allows me to share my mission with the world around me, and most of all it helps celebrate diverse cultural aspects by giving a voice to medical representation. By favoring social media and seeing it as a positive connector, I can highlight the voices of marginalized individuals, to encourage empathy and inspire action. This is when I know that I have made a difference and have been successful in my mission.

Success, to me, is the realization of set goals and the subsequent acknowledgment of their impact on both individuals and the broader community. It's about not only achieving the objectives I've set but also witnessing a tangible shift in awareness and understanding. When the issues I highlight are recognized as pressing and important, and when I see a demonstration of engagement, empathy, and a willingness to see the bigger picture, that is when I know I have truly made a difference. This recognition, both by myself and by the world around me, is the ultimate proof that I have accomplished my goals. It signifies that my efforts have resonated, that the voices I've amplified have been heard, and that the changes I've advocated for are beginning to take root. Success, therefore, is not just about reaching the finish line but about knowing that the journey has brought about meaningful and lasting change.

My future looks bright, and I have high hopes for what is to come as I continue to grow and develop. I envision a future where my ability to connect deeply with people, their stories, and diverse cultures becomes a powerful catalyst for positive change in the world. This unique connection will allow me to bridge gaps between different communities and perspectives, hopefully uniting many along the way. I aspire to use my skills to bring light to the human experience, especially those that deserve more recognition and appreciation. By shining a light on these often-overlooked aspects of humanity, I hope to contribute to a world that values and celebrates the diversity that makes us all unique.

My advice to other young people who want to make a difference is simple: The world needs your passion and innovation. Discover what sparks your interests and channel that energy into something meaningful. It's okay to start small, every action counts. Stay curious, be compassionate, and never underestimate the power of your even smallest action.

Compassion is the one word that describes everything about me. To me, compassion means recognizing and understanding the challenges of others and feeling a desire to help alleviate them. It goes beyond mere sympathy, involving a genuine connection and commitment to supporting others with kindness, empathy, and patience. Compassion sparks a sense of community, strengthens relationships, and promotes a more inclusive and harmonious world by encouraging us to be considerate and supportive of one another. It is with these quotes and my writing that I end my chapter and hope to have inspired you to be more compassionate in everything you do.

"It is not the word that is important, it is the idea and ambition behind it." - Emma Watson

"I love hearing educated people speak and just shut everyone up. Knowledge is always the loudest voice." -Zendaya

"I WISH I KNEW THEN..."

by Lauren LaPointe

Entrepreneur, Philanthropist,
Two-time World Champion Ballroom Dancer,
Creative Business Coach and Motivational Speaker

Looking back on my journey, one-word echoes through every step I've taken: *uncommon*. It's a word my grandfather cherished, and it became my guiding light, even though I didn't realize it at the time. Being *uncommon* meant daring to be different, embracing a path that wasn't laid out for me. But as a young person, I didn't feel *uncommon*—I felt unseen.

As the middle child, I often felt like I had to work harder to earn my place, especially in my family. I wasn't encouraged to dream big or chase after passions. Somehow, I internalized the idea that I had to do something extraordinary to earn my mother's love and approval, and so I held back from pursuing goals for myself. As a result, my childhood wasn't filled with ambitions of greatness; I wasn't a child who dreamt of championships or success. I was simply trying to find my place.

What I didn't know then, and what I wish I had understood, is that *dreams don't have expiration dates*. The spark that flickers within you may seem dim at times, but it never truly goes out. That truth came to life for me in my adulthood. It was then that I rediscovered something I didn't realize I needed: ballroom dancing.

I didn't walk onto that dance floor thinking I was a champion. In fact, I thought the opposite. But I was drawn to it, something inside me reignited, and for the first time, I allowed myself to fully embrace the idea of striving for something without feeling like I had to prove my worth to anyone else. I danced for *me*.

After years of hard work, focus, and dedication, I became a world champion in ballroom dancing within seven years. I wish I had known as a younger version of myself that you don't need anyone else's permission to be great. You don't need to fit into anyone's expectations of you to succeed.

If there's one message I'd want young people to take away from my story, it's this: You don't need to be *common* to find your place in this world. In fact, it's in being *uncommon*—in daring to pursue what calls to you, regardless of the expectations around you—that you will find your true strength.

Don't let the constraints of others' approval dictate how far you go. Your journey might take time, and it might not look like anyone else's, but when you follow what makes you feel alive, greatness will follow. I wish I had known then that what truly makes you exceptional is already within you, waiting to be realized when you dare to be *uncommon*.

CHAPTER 7

#CONFIDENCE
Kevin's One Word

C - create exactly what I want

O - overcome anything that gets in my way

N - never accept defeat

F - fight my fears

I - integrity in everything I do

D – determination

E - empower myself and others

N - new opportunities

C - courage to take the risk

E - engaging with others

THE WINNING MINDSET: ALL YOU NEED TO BUILD CONFIDENCE, CREATE SUCCESS AND FIND FINANCIAL FREEDOM

by Kevin Kyle Keanu Shephard

Drop-Shipper, Content Creator,
Aspiring-Entrepreneur, Mentor

"Procrastination is the assassination of all destinations." -Anonymous

What would you do if it were possible to create what you want, when you want, wherever you want? Growing up, I was surrounded by both good and bad influences. Despite their differences, they all shared a common trait: a strong winning mindset. This environment taught me that with determination and confidence, I could achieve anything I set my mind to. Success isn't about where you come from or what you have; it's about how you think and your willingness to work hard and persevere. This shaped me into who I am today, fueling my mission to inspire and teach others.

As a young entrepreneur, my mission is to inspire and teach kids how to make money from anywhere in the world. By sharing my experiences and practical tips, I aim to help them develop the skills and mindset needed for financial independence. I also strive to support my community by offering guidance and resources to help others achieve their goals and build a better future. I want to show them that with the right skills and mindset, they can achieve financial success no matter who they are or where they come from. However, achieving this requires access to the right knowledge, which often isn't available through traditional education systems. The necessary skills for success are not taught in most schools. Therefore, it's crucial to have the self-discipline to learn these skills on your own. So, where can you learn these skills? Online and through social media.

While most people have a negative opinion about social media or fantasize about other people's lavish lifestyles, they could be focusing on learning how to create that lifestyle for themselves instead of wishing for someone else's, like I did. Social media has had a positive impact on my life, and it's because of it that I have achieved success at such a young age. However, there are many challenges along the way.

One challenge I faced was dealing with my first viral post. Initially exciting, it soon became overwhelming. Despite nearly giving up that night, I decided on a whim to post another video. To my surprise, I woke up the next morning to 90,000 views and $500 in sales. Throughout the day, the sales continued to climb, reaching $12,600 within a few hours. However, I made a serious error in my profit calculations. This mistake cost me around $9,000. I forgot to include the cost of shipping in the profit margin. This experience taught me the importance of truly understanding what you are doing first and not giving up because of your mistakes. Trust me, there will be plenty of them, but persistence and careful planning can help curb their frequency.

A pivotal moment in my life was when I launched my second business. This venture was transformative because it was then that I truly grasped the concept that "your network is your net worth." I began actively connecting with other successful entrepreneurs, and the wealth of knowledge I gained from these interactions was invaluable. As a result, by the age of 15, I was earning between $1,500 and $2,000 per day for almost a month. My success didn't stop there. I started sharing my insights and experiences by speaking on podcasts and hosting Shark Tank-style proposal calls within my Discord community. This platform allowed me to engage with my students directly, further establishing a network of like-minded individuals.

Connecting with like-minded individuals taught me the profound importance of independence and realizing that true happiness doesn't always come from being surrounded by others. It's perfectly okay, and often incredibly fulfilling, to find joy within yourself. In fact, mastering the art of self-contentment is one of the most empowering lessons you can learn at a young age. My journey of self-discovery taught me that being happy alone is not only okay but can also lead to a deeper, more authentic sense of well-being. Learning to enjoy your own company and finding peace within yourself can be one of the most valuable experiences of your life.

This journey of self-discovery was significantly influenced by my environment, which created a winning mindset. I've always looked up to figures like Iman Gadzhi and Jordan Welch, former drop shipping idols, and learned valuable life lessons from them. However, the biggest impact on my life has been my brother, Anthony. His achievements and determination have truly inspired me to keep pushing forward and become a well-invested individual. Additionally, my father has been a constant source of motivation, always encouraging me to work harder in life. He will always be my number one motivator, pushing me to reach my full potential and instilling in me the values of hard work and dedication. His support and belief in me have been instrumental in shaping who I am today.

My view of success goes beyond materialistic possessions. It's not just about new cars, designer clothes, or the latest gadgets. True success, to me, is about having close relationships with family, experiencing the freedom to travel the world, and living without the constant worry of financial constraints. It's about reaching a level of influence where I can inspire those around me to strive for their dreams and realize their potential. I believe the world often places limits on dreams, and I aim to demonstrate that limitless opportunities exist. For me, true success means achieving personal freedom and uplifting others to pursue and achieve their dreams.

My vision for the future is to achieve financial freedom, living comfortably with my family in a peaceful place away from home. I aim to build the largest and most comprehensive drop shipping network and ecosystem, providing valuable resources and support to users worldwide. I want to create a top-notch educational platform that offers accessible and practical classes for aspiring entrepreneurs everywhere. This platform will equip individuals with the knowledge and skills needed to succeed in e-commerce. Ultimately, my goal is to establish a strong and successful business empire in the drop shipping industry. Through hard work and dedication, I hope to make a positive impact and inspire others to achieve their own financial independence.

To young people who want to make a difference, my advice is to start with passion. Identify what truly excites and motivates you, as this will drive your efforts and sustain you through challenges. Educate yourself thoroughly in your chosen field and stay curious. Build a network of like-minded individuals who can offer support, advice, and collaboration opportunities. Be persistent and resilient; setbacks are part of the journey, and learning from them is crucial. Always act with integrity and consider the impact of your actions on others. Lastly, stay adaptable and open to new ideas, as innovation often comes from unexpected places. By combining passion, knowledge, perseverance, and ethics, you can create meaningful change and leave a positive mark on the world.

My one word is "confidence." Confidence means believing in myself and my abilities, even when faced with challenges or uncertainty. It is the foundation for taking risks, making decisions, and pursuing my goals with determination. Confidence empowers me to step out of my comfort zone, embrace new opportunities, and inspire others. It is the key to unlocking my full potential and achieving success in both my personal and professional life.

Some quotes I live by have become guiding principles in my life. "Procrastination is the assassination of all destinations," - unknown. This quote reminds me to take action and not delay my goals. Franklin D. Roosevelt's words, "The only limit to our realization of tomorrow is our doubts of today," inspire me to overcome self-doubt and believe in future possibilities. Winston Churchill's quote, "Success is not final, failure is not fatal: It is the courage to continue that counts," motivates me to persist, knowing that both success and failure are important parts of the journey. Abraham Lincoln's wisdom, "The best way to predict the future is to create it," encourages me to take control of my destiny and actively shape the life I want. Finally, Theodore Roosevelt's statement, "Believe you can and you're halfway there," emphasizes the power of self-belief in achieving my ambitions. Together, these quotes fuel my drive to succeed and shape the way I approach life.

CHAPTER 8

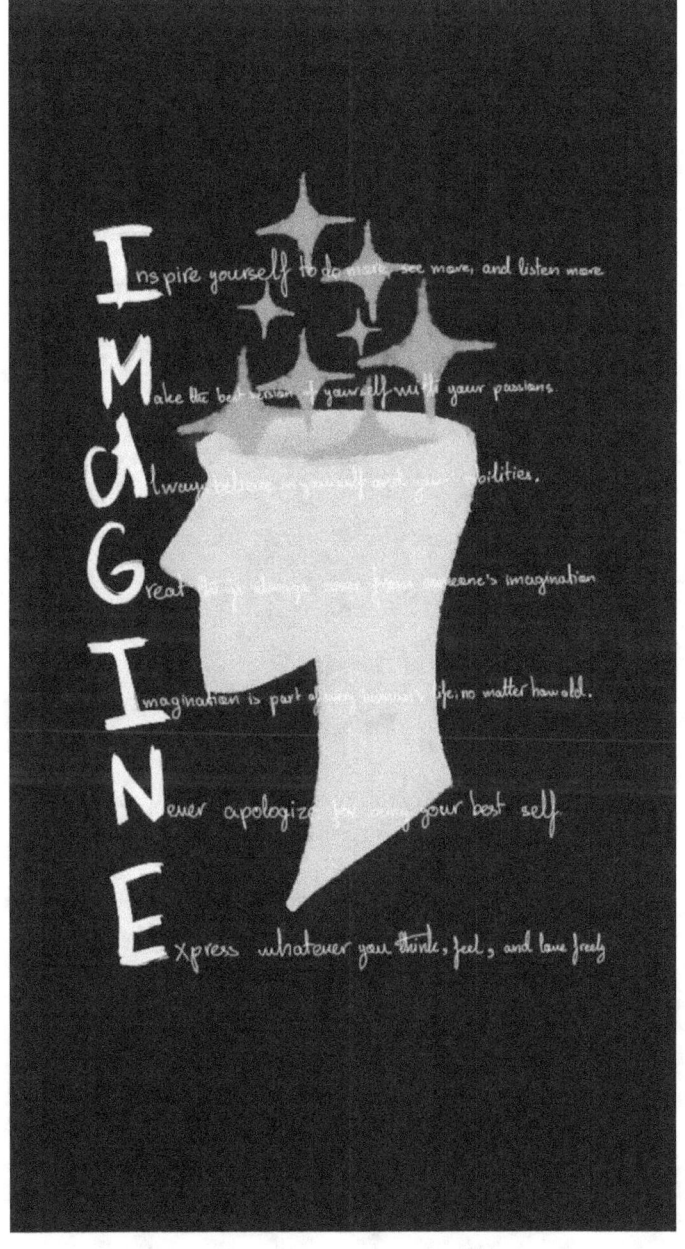

#IMAGINE
Mehrish's One Word

I – inspire yourself to do more, see more, and listen more.

M – make the best version of yourself with your passions.

A – always believe in yourself and your abilities.

G – great things always come from someone's imagination.

I – imagination is a part of every human's life, no matter how old they become.

N – never apologize for being your best self.

E – express whatever you think, feel, and love freely.

MAKING THE WORLD OUR CANVAS

by Mehrish Ali Bokhari

Writer, Artist, Dreamer

"Imagination is more important than knowledge. Knowledge is limited. Imagination encircles the world." ~ *Albert Einstein*

How many children have been told that their imagination will get them nowhere? How many people have lost their imagination because they became too busy? How many people believe that they don't have an imagination? Imagination nowadays, at least from what I see online, seems to be undervalued. Why imagine when AI can do it all for you? To many people, imagining things and using your imagination is a waste of time. In today's world, everything is about the grind, whether for fame, money, or power. Life has become meaningless thanks to this "grind." Many children now are raised to drown themselves in their academics, to never write a story unless it's for a school task, to never draw unless it's "making some money." When you read this chapter, know one thing: a human being is nothing without imagination.

Don't let anyone tell you that imagination will get you nowhere in life!

My mission is to become a doctor that people can trust, that people look for, and a doctor that people can leave from feeling seen, heard, and well-treated. Doctors can be arrogant sometimes, often refusing to admit that they are wrong. This makes a lot of people distrust doctors, and sometimes this arrogance turns into medical malpractice, which claims the lives of 400,000 people each year. I do not want to be a doctor who contributes to this statistic. I hope to help people feel seen and heard when they enter my office, and I hope to treat my patients in the best way possible.

I have many qualities that will help me along the way. My strong comprehension skills will be a great asset in medical school, helping me absorb and retain the vast amount of information required for my studies. Additionally, my ability to identify micro expressions and my good social skills will be invaluable when interacting with patients, allowing me to understand and respond to their needs effectively. I'm also a quick learner who rarely repeats mistakes, which will serve me well both in treating patients and navigating the challenges of medical school. However, I believe my greatest skill is my imagination, which will enable me to think creatively and approach problems from unique perspectives.

Now let's look at imagination and social media. I believe that social media is what you make of it. If you have an online business, social media is one of the best ways to advertise. However, if you don't have a business, then I really think there is no need to have a lot of social media accounts. Social media distracts us from our lives, hence the term "doomscrolling," referring to scrolling mindlessly for hours and hours on TikTok, Instagram, and YouTube Shorts. Social media also compels a lot of people to try stupid things like drugs, alcohol, and weird trends or "pranks." For a lot of other people, including myself, it desensitizes us to the rest of the world. Social media has, thus far, been the bane of my existence. It prevents me from enjoying my hobbies; it cuts down on my sleep; it makes me forget to eat; it makes me forget to drink water; it makes me forget to take care of myself in general. I don't even have that many social media accounts. I only have Pinterest, YouTube, and WhatsApp. Scrolling on my Pinterest "For You" page, scrolling on YouTube Shorts, and constantly checking WhatsApp for messages has wasted a lot of my time and has significantly decreased my attention span. It happens to everyone who has social media, even those who have businesses online. Social media is the bane of imagination, rotting away your attention span and ability to be productive.

My biggest challenge in life was preparing for my final IGCSE Islamiyat and Pakistan Studies exams. These were my weakest subjects since I had been studying in the IB system for my entire life, so I had to put in extra effort during my studies for the exams. It was extremely difficult, and I often found myself stress eating or procrastinating. I overcame this struggle by sucking it up and continuing to study despite my many grievances. In the end, I was able to complete my IB exams and the Islamiyat and Pakistan Studies exams with little to no issues. I stayed motivated by remembering that I would not be able to become a doctor if my MYP grades were not high. That kept me from letting myself fail.

Success to me is being able to live contentedly. You should be able to know when to say "enough" and not fall into the corporate trap of consumerism and end up buying things you know you don't need. You are also successful when you can follow your dreams to get the profession you want, the life you want, the family you want, etc. When you can follow your dreams and live contentedly, then no matter how much you earn, you are successful.

My vision for the future has many different facets, but the goal is to do better so I can help my country. I want to live in a different country than Pakistan, preferably remaining within the continent. I have two places in mind: Finland and Japan. Both countries have beautiful beaches and mountain landscapes, but Finland has a better work environment, and the euro is stronger than the yen. I am still weighing my options, but the main idea is that I want to live in a better country than Pakistan so that I can help Pakistan. I plan to raise enough money to be able to build hospitals in rural areas all over Pakistan, especially on the western side of Pakistan and the northern mountains. These hospitals will be of little to no cost (to attend or stay in), but the technology, service, and courtesy will be the best of the best. I know it is ambitious, but rural areas really need better medical facilities, and I feel that if I try hard enough, I will be able to provide them.

If I were to give advice to other young people my age, it would be to always try. Even if it's just once, try. The first time I tried to make a Roblox game, I failed miserably. The second time I tried (and I am still trying) to make it, it turned out exactly how I was hoping it would. The best thing about trying it once and leaving it is that you build up the patience to try again later. You will get an opportunity one day to try again when you feel like it. Just remember you will never know if you like something or not unless you try.

My One Word is Imagine. Imagining and imagination, in general, are very important to me because they feed my hobbies, and they prevent me from feeling bored. I feel that a lot of people are losing their imagination because of how easy it is for others to imagine for them, and because of that, a lot of people live their lives on autopilot. Imagination is a core part of childhood, but the majority of the time, parents squash any bit of it they can find for multiple reasons. I will share one reason here: they don't want their kids to go into careers that use imagination, like movie production, art, or writing, because these careers are, in their opinion, "useless." So, I really hope this chapter inspires people and encourages them to imagine and never stop using their imagination.

The following are quotes I live by that bring imagination into perspective:

"Happiness is not an ideal of reason, but of imagination."
~ Immanuel Kant

"Imagination is more important than knowledge. Knowledge is limited. Imagination encircles the world." ~ Albert Einstein

"Opportunities pass like clouds." ~ Imam Ali ibn Abi Talib (a.s)

CHAPTER 9

#GROWTH
Shrusti's One Word

G - goal setting - setting clear goals & working towards them

R - resilience - bounce back from challenges

O - open-minded - embracing new ideas

W - work ethic - putting in consistent efforts

T - time management -prepare a schedule and follow it strictly

H - helping others - supporting & uplifting others on their journey

A VISION OF GROWTH AND EMPOWERMENT

by Shrusti Mhetre

Entrepreneur, Mentor, Advocate for Financial Independence

"Never go with the flow because you never know when your moment of opportunity will arise." - Shrusti Mhetre

Here I would like to share my journey toward achieving financial independence, not just for myself but for others as well. We all face challenges in finding this type of freedom, and often people do not have the skills or knowledge necessary to know where to turn for support. From leveraging the power of social media for personal and professional growth to overcoming the hurdles brought on by the COVID-19 pandemic, I aim to inspire the readers of my story to pursue their goals with resilience, determination, and an open mind.

My main goal is to achieve financial independence for myself, while also helping others achieve the same. I am particularly focused on assisting students in developing their skills and enabling them to start earning on their own. I've noticed that there are many individuals who have a strong desire to work on themselves and achieve financial security. However, they often struggle to find the perfect platform to begin their journey. That's where I come in! I want to provide the best possible platform for people to grow and thrive in their lives.

To contribute to the world and make a difference, I am actively involved in different activities which I feel are important because there are so many important causes that need our help in the world today. I have contributed to this world by being a part of SaveSoil by SadhGuru, where we plant trees and educate people on the importance of plants so that they will plant one as well. While I love helping all causes, my greatest passion lies in helping other young people develop skills to earn money. I am actively involved in helping students acquire new skills and knowledge through offline conferences. These conferences serve as a platform for individuals to share their expertise and learn from one another. By facilitating this knowledge exchange and practical implementation, we can empower students to succeed in their chosen paths.

Social media has indeed emerged as a powerful platform for personal and professional growth. It has provided incredible opportunities for entrepreneurship and project development. The global reach of social media allows people from all over the world to connect, collaborate, and share ideas.

While social media offers numerous benefits, it's important to acknowledge that there are both positive and negative aspects to it. On one hand, it enables us to connect with others, share experiences, and discover new ideas. It serves as a platform for self-expression and community building. In fact, Instagram has played a significant role in my journey, by allowing me to provide others with opportunities and support.

Social media platforms like Instagram also offer valuable knowledge through features like reels, which can help individuals focus on life, online skill development courses, yoga, and more. It's all about finding a balance and using social media in a way that enriches our lives without becoming overwhelming or harmful.
Many people have successfully built careers through social media, utilizing platforms like Instagram, Facebook, LinkedIn, and others. It's remarkable how individuals can earn money and achieve financial independence through these platforms.

During the trying times of the COVID-19 pandemic, I faced numerous hurdles that tested my resilience. Like many others, I grappled with financial strains, especially regarding my education and basic needs. However, these challenges spurred me to pursue self-sufficiency, not only for myself but also to support my family and aid others facing similar hardships. In the midst of pandemic adversity, I dedicated myself to personal growth and extending assistance to those in need. My primary aim is to empower students, recognizing the pivotal role financial stability plays in their educational pursuits and overall well-being. By fostering independence among students, I aspire to alleviate their financial burdens, enabling them to pursue their academic aspirations with confidence.

My vision as an entrepreneur is not only to achieve financial independence by the age of 25, but also to help students like us develop their skills and become financially independent. I want to provide education and inspiration to people, guiding them towards leading independent lives and pursuing their dreams. By sharing knowledge and support, I hope to make a positive impact in the world of entrepreneurship, empowering individuals to navigate their own paths to success. It's all about helping others and making a difference.

My vision includes the goal of enabling students to achieve financial independence even before completing their education, allowing them to embark on their professional journeys with confidence and financial stability. By providing the necessary guidance and resources, I aspire to create a platform that equips students with the skills and knowledge needed to thrive both academically and financially. I want to make this vision a reality and empower a new generation of independent and successful individuals.

My one word is *GROWTH*, and it embodies everything I strive for in my life. Growth, to me, begins with *Goal setting*— establishing clear objectives and diligently working toward them. It's about understanding where I want to go and creating a roadmap to get there. Along this journey, *Resilience* plays a crucial role, as it's essential to bounce back from challenges and setbacks with renewed determination. I also believe that *Open-*

mindedness is a key component of growth, as it involves embracing new ideas, perspectives, and opportunities that can expand my horizons and help me evolve. A strong **Work** *ethic* is fundamental to achieving growth, as it requires putting in consistent effort and dedication, even when the path is difficult. Hand in hand with this is *Time management*—preparing a schedule and following it strictly to ensure that every moment is used effectively and contributes to my progress. Lastly, growth isn't just about personal achievement; it's also about *Helping others* by supporting and uplifting them on their journeys. By doing so, I believe we can all grow together, creating a community where everyone thrives.

"Be Educated, Be Organized, and Be Agitated." - Dr. B.R. Ambedkar

"Anyone can give up; it's the easiest thing in the world to do. But to hold it together when everyone else would understand if you fell apart, that's true strength." - Viktor E. Frankl

"Never go with the flow because you never know when your moment of opportunity will arise." - Shrusti Mhetre

"I WISH I KNEW THEN..."
Inherited Wealth: The Legacy of Education and Will

by Jona Lemmonds

Founder of Launch Your Wealth
Business Investor, Wealth Creation Mentor, Speaker

"Making an impact in entrepreneurship, wealth and success is an outcome when you are intentional to serve and do good for others, not just for yourself." – Jona Lemmonds

My parents were the pioneers of academic and education achievement in their families, bridging the gap from elementary-educated parents to college educated professionals. They were children of post-famine, post-World War II parents who had only been able to reach grade four literacy level but who worked diligently to secure a better future for their children. From a young age, my parents grasped that education was not just a milestone—it was a means to freedom, a promise of financial independence, and an access to a life beyond their circumstances.

My father was a prime example of not letting his situation and where he came from determine his future. He was naturally interested in reading, writing, and a knack for conversations. With his resilience, he defined his generation. The first in his family tree to have accomplished a master's degree in arts & history and completed a Law degree. He juggled jobs, bartered skills, and tutored peers just to exchange for a place to sleep temporarily until he had saved up some money to secure his own room and board at the university, forgoing comforts many take for granted. Where others had family support and financial means, he had real life experience, a network of goodwill, and determination. He crafted his own success moving from tutoring for a bed to sleep on, to advising political candidates, becoming a legal counsel for Fortune 500 companies like Coca-Cola, and offering pro bono work to those in need. His journey was a testament to the idea that while education opened the door, his tenacity was what walked him through it.

My mother's path, too, was marked by a strong determination to break free from her family's cycle of factory work making equivalent to $2.00 per month in the 1940's era. Watching her older siblings take on responsibilities from a young age, she saw education as her gateway to autonomy and choice. Her parents, always busy with 12-hour shifts at a cookie factory, believed a stable job was successful enough, but my mother wanted more—the freedom to create her own path. She pursued a bachelor's degree in business administration, transforming the knowledge she gained into a life filled with opportunity that led her to have a career and travel abroad. Her education was a vehicle to leave behind the predictable life of labor, and opened the experiences that eventually led her own family to build a life with confidence, direction and financial independence.

As I came of age, my own educational experience offered options that my parents could never have imagined back in their time. Though we didn't have the internet, Google, LinkedIn, YouTube or ChatGPT in the 80's and 90's era, we had co-op programs, hands-on classes, and extracurriculars. I loved exploring cooking, sewing, and woodworking. By junior high, I understood that these activities were opening my mind in ways beyond books and grades. By high school, I wanted to check my limits, if there were such? Not out of competition but out of a curiosity about what I could explore, discover and achieve if I tried everything that called to me. The voices of my parents were there, whispering reminders of the privilege I now held, the freedoms they'd worked to secure, and the legacy they are passing down but expected for me to continue. As I became an adult, got married and had my own children, it is when I realized that my parents did not have expectations -- they just truly valued their experience and hard work in getting an education, using it as a way to get what they wanted. And the *A-ha moment* clicked, and stayed in me as a reminder that what matters the most is what I do with the education, to use it to create, build and expand what I want to have in my life. High school was a turning point. I excelled, not as a straight-A student, but with a drive that kept me on the honor roll and fueled my love for language arts, music, and French class. Math may have intimidated me, but I took ownership of my learning experience, seeking out new challenges and testing my own perceived limits. Rather than focusing on what I wanted to "be" when I grew up, I became captivated by the idea of what I could "become." By high school graduation, I felt ready to see what was out there, whether it was college, getting on the workforce, or both.

At 18 years old, I took a year off, working odd jobs to learn more about myself and determine whether a usual route like most students who are off to college, was even the best route for me at that time. While my parents had dreams for me of law, medicine, or accounting, they supported my decision without judgment. I saved some money from my odd part time jobs, a receptionist at a luxury furniture shop, and as an assistant helper at a children's daycare that bought my airfare and spending money. The plan was for four weeks that became four months. It was one of the best decisions I made. Within that year, I told a friend that I am looking for a job and she asked if I'd consider working for a bank -- I said yes without hesitation. Curiosity at its best! I was hired that same week, and just like that, little did I know that my journey in the world of finance began. From day one, I was ready to go. I became intrigued and interested in customer service, banking management, and financial systems -- it led me to the transformative power of knowledge. The career that unfolded was not what I—or my parents—had anticipated, but I knew that first week, it was where I belonged.

Looking back from where I stand today, deep in the world of entrepreneurship, immersed in the business industry, and the ebb and flow of the wealth scene, I realize how much there is I would tell my younger self of what I know now. I've crossed paths with people from every walk of life, absorbing lessons from each encounter and pursuing self-awareness as passionately as I once pursued education. The journey was anything but smooth; 80% of the time, twists and turns, highs and lows but I was on a steady path, and the 20%, I was learning from what was going well. I found it more worthwhile to focus on what worked and let go of what didn't. The key is to identify and admit what is holding us back, or no longer is a positive contribution to our goals, and well-being; to simply focus on optimizing life -- *progress over perfection.*

My parents set a powerful foundation, but I had to pave my own path—one paved not just with successes but with all the mistakes that taught me just as much. They taught me resilience and instilled in me a desire for knowledge, truth and strength, but it was up to me to break through any potential limits, and define what success meant in my own version, on my own terms. The legacy they passed down I carry forward— not just as in a career or a title, not merely as a wealth or societal approval, but as a mission. It's about creating impact, lifting others through my work, my business, my experiences. It's about moving forward, holding tight to the many possibilities before me, and making my own mark in this lifetime.

Seeds of Wealth:
Life Education, Self-Education and School Education

School and formal education open doors to countless opportunities, equipping us with knowledge and credentials that can help pave the way in academia, careers, and professional pursuits. But beyond the accolades and degrees, beyond the coursework, there lies a deeper journey—one we must take upon ourselves. True growth comes when we invest time and energy into *life education*, building real-world skills, gaining hands-on experience, and diving into *inner-self work* that strengthens our mindset, our spirit, the emotional intelligence and capacity.

Life teaches us what textbooks cannot: the power of having mentors, the value of a supportive network, and the insights that come from being part of a community. These elements, alongside the broader exposure to the world's diversity, help us navigate the competitiveness, chaos, and uncertainties that await us. Education is our vehicle, but it's the ecosystem around it—the mentors, experiences, self-discovery—that gives it purpose, direction, and depth. With all three forms of education—life, self, and school—we're equipped to not just move forward but to thrive, make a difference, share our talents and gifts.

Beyond the Education, Career, and Money: Unlock and Create Inner Wealth
I wish I knew then...

Our school systems did not teach us how to embark on self-directed study or foster the frameworks for continuous personal growth. Over the past three decades, I've gathered invaluable experiences, not only from formal education but also from observing people, navigating unique challenges, and solving problems that inevitably arise in life. My journey in both the professional industry and entrepreneurship has been a platform to witness a spectrum of ideas, beliefs, personalities, and life stories. What I've come to realize is that *listening*—truly hearing people—has been one of my greatest strengths, that I thought was because I did not have much to say, or I was a shy highschool student. It has become a formula for me to communicate effectively, understand how I can be of help, and strategize solutions that can make an impact.

Working with people from diverse backgrounds —from those with high school diplomas to PhDs, on projects small and large, from startup ventures to multimillion-dollar opportunities—has taught me that success comes from a combination of openness, adaptability, and a willingness to learn from others. When I started my path to building my businesses many years ago, and started my own company in 2022, I had no investors or a safety net to begin with. What I did have was a belief in the power of combining experience, knowledge, and the attitude of resilience. With the right mix of energy, time, and effort, my business started growing, and I grew right alongside it.

These are lessons drawn from my past, refined in the present, and shared with hope for the future.

Self-Study and Lifelong Learning
Embrace learning beyond the classroom. True education comes from immersing yourself in life, observing, and adapting.

Listening as a Superpower
Listening unlocks understanding. It enables connection, empowers solutions, and opens doors to meaningful opportunities.

Diversity of Experiences
Engage with people from all backgrounds and professions; each encounter brings fresh insights, a new perspective, or a lesson that will serve you in the long run.

The Value of Building from Ground
Starting without money, or investors teaches resilience and creativity. Building from the ground up with a solid vision and the right attitude builds not just a business, or company, but character.

Continuous Growth

As your work grows, so do you. Each challenge, victory, and setback are an opportunity to expand and develop into your greatest potential.

In addition, more importantly, these lessons reveal that true wealth is in the experiences, insights, and processes that we accumulate, transcending education, career, and money.

The inner wealth we build that ultimately shapes our lives and influences the future we want to create starts with the inner self.

Core Belief and Faith: The Oxygen of Life

Faith as Foundation: Faith is essential, like oxygen. It sustains your spirit and resilience, allowing you to thrive beyond mere existence.

Belief in Yourself: Start by believing in yourself; don't rely on others to validate your worth or abilities.

Higher Connection: Faith exists within you, even if you don't fully understand it. It's there to connect with God, the Universe, or the source of higher power, bringing strength and guidance.

Self-Awareness: Your Ever-Growing Power

Growth is Constant: Growth unfolds in stages, with many moments, seasons, and years passing quickly. Be present in each, as these experiences build the wisdom that will serve you, your family, your community, and many other people around you.

Take In Every Moment: The power of self-awareness allows you to inspire, elevate, and empower not only yourself but those around you, work with you, and trust you, creating a legacy of insight and meaning.

Perception: Redefining Success, Money, and Wealth

Success: Success is the journey—the process you commit to as you strive to achieve meaningful goals.

Money: Money is an outcome, reflecting the effort, creativity, and value you bring into the world.

Wealth: True wealth is about values and beliefs, unlocking possibilities beyond material things, and offering a fulfilling, purpose-driven life.

Values and Principles: Your True North

Value System: Dedicate time to reflect on and shape your personal values. Your values will help you design the life you desire and define the person you want to become.

Anchor in Principles: Build and refine principles to ground you in a world that is busy, demanding, and aggressive. Let these principles guide your decisions and actions. And it can shine light when difficult and challenging times happen.

Dream - Imagine - Believe: The Power of Your Inner Vision

Embrace Your Ideas and Desires: Your dreams and desires are your own; they are the intuitive voice within, urging you to reach for more.

Resist Scarcity and Doubt: Scarcity thinking and self-doubt aren't meant for you. Trust that you have the power to shape your life and achieve your deepest aspirations.

Limitations Are Not Real: It is only there if and when you think it is. The limitations do not exist. You hold the inner wealth that will lead in creating the life you want, and more.

CHAPTER 10

#PEACE

Vasundhara's One Word

P- Promise of harmony and light

E- Empathy for each living being around

A- Always show gratitude to universe

C- Compassion in the heart

E- Enduring hope and faith

AMIDST RUINS, INNER PEACE PREVAILS....

by Vasundhara Chaudhary

Mental Health Advocate, Change-Maker,
Leader, Public Speaker

"When you want something, all the universe conspires in helping you to achieve it." - Paulo Coelho's The Alchemist

In a world that doesn't understand that mental health is as important as your physical health, my mission is to spread awareness about mental health and break the stigma attached to it. My journey started long back during the pandemic when my mental health worsened, and I realized that I had no one to approach for help. Even if I would have approached, people wouldn't have taken the issue seriously because I already heard people saying...." There's nothing like anxiety and depression!! It's just a strategy to grab attention." This was the turning point, and I realized the importance of how the young generation needs to be educated about the same and I started Inspire dose. A youth organization that aimed to spread awareness using social media platforms, podcasts and magazines, we released health care journal sheets, conducted surveys and started giving free counseling sessions by collaborating with psychologists. I want to build a community where people take care of their mental health the way they take care of their physical health. Be a spiritual being by connecting to the universe. Invest in their self-care and be an empathetic being.

According to me it depends on how you are using social media. It can be both a boon and curse. During the pandemic, social media was the only platform to create awareness and that was the time I realized that social media can be used for your personal growth and to connect with like-minded people. It can also be used for the betterment of the world. I had connected and collaborated with people around the globe solely with the help of social media. I had attended a lot of webinars and workshops which helped me in my holistic development. Social media has a lot of potential always remember "Scroll with purpose: Seek inspiration, not distraction"

I got inspiration from my grandfather who is a doctor and has been working for the betterment of the people by giving treatment at nominal charges in rural areas. Seeing him working selflessly in a profession where he can earn a lot of money hit me really hard. Secondly when my mental health worsened, I thought of millions of other people who are suffering from mental health issues and have no support. One can't realize others' pain until one has gone through it himself. For me success is neither something materialistic nor something that can be achieved. Since childhood we have been told about various milestones that we should achieve, and this will further decide our success. But I feel that is all temporary, you reach one milestone, and the next one is already waiting for you. I feel success is in small daily wins. Every step you take towards your milestone defines your success. If you made someone smile today by helping them in some way that is also an example of success as you were successful in being a generous human. I would like each one of you to sit down every day at night and write down your #successmoments of the day and this will definitely boost your confidence and give you a sense of fulfillment.

I aspire to pursue my career in the field of psychiatry as that is something that I feel deeply connected with. I want to make a change in the field of mental health and break the stigma attached to it. These are the visions I have for my professional growth but as I stated in the starting, we should never forget ourselves. I want to explore new places, try new cuisines, try new hobbies, read a variety of books, understand new cultures and meet new people. At the same time, I need to stay connected to my roots and the universe.

The first thing you need to do to get started is discover the thing that interests you most, something that fills you up with passion and you can dedicate your whole life for that cause. Then start taking small steps in that direction. Don't think of the number of people that got impacted or your success rate. Even if you have impacted one individual it is considered to be success only. Always remember that life is like a wave. Sometimes you are at crest and sometimes at trough but what is more important is you should keep going and never give up.

Some tips to take care of mental health.

Here is an acrostic for the word MENTAL HEALTH:

M-Meditation
E-Exercise
N-No to negativity
T-Take a break
A-Accept who you are
L-Listen soothing music

H- Healthy Lifestyle
E-Eat well
A-Ask for help
L-Laugh loudly
T-Take Deep breath
H-Hone your talents

Being an avid observer, I wrote this poem. Giving all examples of nature that show how when there is no spark of hope but at the end everything comes out bright and full of light! The poem is full of imagery!

Spark a light of hope!

Whenever you feel there is no hope left!
Remember on a foggy day the sun, the moon and stars also had no hope!
Remember in the winter season the snow-covered grassland also had no hope!
Remember in the autumn season the tree without any leaf also had no hope!
Remember the caterpillar who was about to become a butterfly also had no hope!
But all of them shined, blossomed, bloomed and bounced back in an incredible manner!
Just because they still had faith in themselves and the almighty!
There's always sunshine after a storm!
You just have to be faithful and patient!

PEACE!

Peace is my one word. Peace is a calm and gentle feeling that helps us stay balanced and happy. It's when our minds and hearts are free from worry and stress. When we feel peaceful, we can handle challenges better and enjoy life more fully. Peace comes from within and can be found even in the busiest or toughest times.

In the midst of ruins, where everything feels lost, inner peace still stands strong. It's in the quiet moments between the destruction that we find calm and comfort. Even when everything seems to be falling apart, this inner peace helps us stay grounded and find a sense of stillness.

I would ask you all to "Find your own peace and let it be your guide."

I leave you with quotes that have inspired me on my journey:

"You have the right to perform your duty, but you are not entitled to the fruits of your actions."
> *- Chapter 2, Verse 47, Bhagavad Gita.*

"When you want something, all the universe conspires in helping you to achieve it."
> *- Paulo Coelho's The Alchemist.*

"Even the darkest night will end, and the sun will rise"
> *- Victor Hugo's Les Misérables*

"The only way to find peace is to let go of your attachment to the world and embrace the present moment."
> *- Michael A. Singer's The Untethered Soul*

CHAPTER 11

#FAITH

Jadon's One Word

F - fortitude

A - acceptance

I - integrity

T - tenacity

H – happiness

MY TESTIMONY WITH FAITH

by Jadon Lemmonds

Student, Athlete, Leader, Mentor, Christian

"Faith is taking the first step even when you don't see the whole staircase."
- Dr. Martin Luther King, Jr.

I was born and raised in a family where Christianity was an integral part of everyday life. My family attended church every Sunday, and religious holidays were celebrated with great importance and joy. Growing up, I participated in youth groups and various church activities and attended private schools that emphasized God's love and teachings. Faith in God and Jesus Christ was a tradition deeply engraved in my family's culture and lifestyle. Yet, as I grew older, I began to question the beliefs I had been taught and sought understanding beyond what I had been raised to believe.

In my teenage years in high school, I encountered people with diverse beliefs. Exposure to different ideas and perspectives made me question my own faith. Why do I believe in God? Who is Jesus, really? What if there is no higher power? These doubts grew louder, and by the end of my sophomore year, I had distanced myself from the faith of my childhood. I delved into seeking answers in a secular world and relied on logic and reason for reassurance. While logic provided solace, there was always a lingering sense of emptiness that reason alone could not fill.

During a challenging period in my sophomore and junior years, I experienced faltering faith. Personal setbacks and inner conflicts led to moments of reflection and efforts to find myself. I felt I was declining in my sports and my grades, and I went through rough patches with the people around me. Despite my pursuit of solutions to my problems, I realized I had neglected the spiritual side of my life. The very questions that had driven me away from faith now led me back to God and my roots. I began to reconnect with God as well as put in time to reflect on myself, finding myself again in the process. Conversations with mentors, attending various church services, and spending time working on my goals were part of this journey. Though it was not easy and was filled with moments of doubt, there were also moments of profound clarity and peace. Through these experiences, I began to feel God's presence once more and began to rebuild faith in both Him and myself.

Rebuilding my faith was like piecing together a shattered glass. Each fragment represented a different aspect of my journey. I learned that faith in God was not about having all the answers but embracing the mystery and trusting in His divine plan. Faith in Him led to a stronger sense of trust in myself as I felt I was on the right path. I learned that faith could coexist with doubt; questioning could lead to deeper understanding. Reconnecting with my community was also significant. Finding people who helped push me out of my comfort zone and helped me work harder reminded me that it is always important to put faith in others as well, especially those who want to see you win. Success is never achieved alone!

Today, I continue to grow my faith in all aspects of life: faith in myself during hard times, faith in those around me, and, personally, faith in God. I have come to understand that faith is not static; it grows and changes as we do. The more we experience and learn, the stronger our faith in ourselves becomes. It is a source of strength and comfort in times of trouble and can often make or break you. Instilling faith was not a single moment of revelation but a continuous journey of rediscovery, breaking and rebirthing trust in my life. It taught me that faith is not about having all the answers but about being open to the unknown and trusting in a bigger purpose.

Faith in oneself is equally important as everything else we do to reach our goals. Believing in our abilities and trusting in our journey empowers us to face life's challenges with confidence. Faith in oneself involves recognizing our strengths, acknowledging our worth, and understanding that we have the power to overcome obstacles and achieve our goals. Combining faith in God with faith in oneself helped me create a sense of resilience that aids me in overcoming fear. Knowing how strong you are, as well as staying true to your dreams, can navigate you through the ups and downs of life. Although it won't make the journey easier, it will definitely make the goal achievable.

In my life, faith has shown its profound impact on all areas of life. From fostering deeper, more loving relationships to providing strength and resilience in the face of challenges, faith offers a sense of purpose and connection that transcends individual struggles. When you have faith in something bigger than yourself—whether it's Jesus, another religious belief, a broader spiritual understanding, or knowing we are all part of a community—it helps you navigate life's complexities with hope and compassion. It reminds you that you are part of a larger story, encouraging you to live with love, integrity, and a commitment to making a positive difference in the world. Embracing this broader perspective enriches your life, grounding you in a sense of meaning and community that sustains you through all of life's ups and downs.

Faith, whether in God or in oneself, is about trust. It is about finding peace amidst chaos and hope in the face of despair. As Dr. Martin Luther King, Jr. once said, "Faith is taking the first step even when you don't see the whole staircase." It is not only belief but also courage, knowing that what you are doing is part of a greater purpose. My journey with faith, with all its twists and turns, has shown me that I am not weak but resilient and capable of finding strength in both the seen and the unseen.

So, what does faith do in one's life? As my faith has grown, I've come to understand that it's a journey that involves both the heart and the mind. It's not about accepting things without question; rather, it's a process of in-depth, personal growth that raises questions and doubts. For me, faith is a continual conversation with God, a relationship that is dynamic and ever-changing as I learn more about myself and the world around me. Faith doesn't only need to be with God; it can also be about believing in oneself and one's own abilities. The inner dialogue with yourself and your soul can lead you to realize your true strength in facing challenges and understanding your weaknesses, as well as finding answers to your questions.

As I've said before, faith isn't only something related to God, but it is deeply connected with our own individual lives as well. Many successful people, such as Tom Brady, Jeff Bezos, and David Goggins, all became successful because of the faith they had in their abilities and strengths. Everyone goes through problems; what separates those who are resilient and those who aren't is the faith and trust they have in their lives. When you lack trust in yourself, you have already lost.

One of the most profound lessons I've learned is that faith is a source of resilience. During times of uncertainty and challenge, it offers a sense of hope and strength. It's not about having all the answers but about trusting that there is a greater plan at work, even when we can't see it clearly. In my own life, this trust allows me to face difficulties with a sense of peace, knowing that I am supported by a loving God. It's this trust that helps me navigate the ups and downs of high school life, with all its pressures and uncertainties. For you, if the resilience doesn't come from God, it can come from the trust in a successful future, a bigger purpose, or an overall path in life that you have planned for your life.

Community has played a crucial role in my faith journey.

Finding a church that values question and encourages exploration has been transformative. Being part of a faith community provides a sense of belonging and support. We share our joys and struggles, lift each other up, and grow together in our understanding of God's love. This communal aspect of faith reminds me that we are not meant to walk this path alone. We are connected by our shared beliefs and our desire to live out the teachings of Jesus. Community can also mean the people we choose to surround ourselves with—our friends, family, school, or workplace. Those around us can remind us of our own strengths and weaknesses and can uplift us, pushing us to be a better version of ourselves. A question to ask yourself is this: "Do I have a community that I can remain faithful to, that can help me in my journey through life?"

Ultimately, faith is about love—whether it's God's love for us, our love for others, or even the love we have for ourselves. It's about living a life that reflects this love in our actions and interactions. Personally, I love to incorporate the teachings of Jesus in my own examples of faith. Jesus' teachings emphasize compassion, forgiveness, and selflessness, and striving to embody these values has brought a deeper sense of fulfillment and joy to my life. Faith is not a destination but a journey, one that I continue to walk with an open heart and encourage you to do as well. Through faith, I find purpose, connection, and a profound sense of peace that sustains me. A question to ask yourself is this: "Do I incorporate a faithful and loving heart in everything I do, accepting everyone with an open mind and heart?"

Faith has the power to transform relationships by fostering deeper connections rooted in love and understanding. As a teenager, navigating friendships and family dynamics can be challenging, but faith provides a foundation of compassion and empathy. It taught me to see others through the lens of love, giving me the patience and forgiveness needed to strengthen my bonds with others. When you approach your relationships with faith, you'll find that conflicts are easier to resolve, and bonds grow stronger. This sense of love and acceptance creates a supportive network where everyone feels valued and understood, enriching your social experiences and providing a sense of belonging.

Moreover, faith plays a significant role in achieving success by instilling values such as perseverance, integrity, and a positive mindset. It helps you stay focused on your goals and maintain a sense of purpose, even when faced with obstacles. Faith encourages you to believe in your abilities and trust that with hard work and determination, you can overcome challenges. It also reminds you that success is not just about personal achievement but about making a positive impact on the world around you. By grounding your actions in faith, you strive to pursue excellence not only for your benefit but also to contribute to the well-being of others, creating a ripple effect of love and positive change.

Faith can help you become more successful. Believing that there is a grand design for your life can give you the courage to pursue your dreams with confidence. This belief helps you see beyond immediate challenges and keeps you motivated to push through difficulties. It provides a sense of direction and assurance that your efforts are part of a larger plan.

Faith in either God or a bigger purpose (or both!) in your life can transform your approach to success. It encourages you to align your actions with your values, pursue goals that contribute to the greater good, and remain resilient in the face of adversity. By doing so, you'll find that your journey is not only more fulfilling but also more impactful, leaving a lasting legacy of love, compassion, and positive change. We are always part of a "bigger picture" and have significance in our lives. Trust that we are always on the right path when we line ourselves up with what is good, and always have faith in yourself and your journey.

The F.A.I.T.H Acronym

To me, faith isn't only a word but an acronym that reminds me about the traits needed to live strong and successful in my everyday life. It has personally helped me overcome fear and cowardice in many situations in life, such as in my sports games, relationships, or life opportunities, and I feel it could help others with their own obstacles. Faith is the acronym for:

Fortitude - the act of courage in pain or adversity. Fortitude is the strength of mind and spirit that enables you to endure adversity with courage and resilience. It involves facing challenges with a resilient mindset and seeing obstacles as growth opportunities. By embracing perseverance, setting small goals, and staying consistent, you build a foundation of inner strength to face life's highs and lows.

Acceptance - the hardest one to learn to incorporate in life. Acceptance is the companion to fortitude, allowing you to face challenges with an open heart and mind. It's not giving up but acknowledging circumstances as they are, allowing you to move forward purposefully. Acceptance helps you learn from difficulties, embrace differences, and remain open to growth by being coachable and flexible.

Integrity - the backbone of success in any aspect of life. Integrity is about having a strong sense of truth and morals, and consistently doing what is right, even when it's challenging. Defining your core principles and practicing honesty and accountability encourages a reputation of reliability and self-respect.

Tenacity - the willpower that keeps you on track. It is the willpower to pursue goals despite obstacles. Tenacity, when coupled with faith, becomes a powerful force in your journey toward success. Aligning your actions with your beliefs and maintaining a hopeful mindset allows you to overcome difficulties, trusting that struggles contribute to growth and purpose.

Happiness - the true riches of life. Living in happiness doesn't mean you will always win, but it is being able to see the treasure in every moment of your life. Happiness is the lasting fulfillment that comes from appreciating life's moments and learning from both joys and struggles. Practicing gratitude, affirming self-worth, and surrounding yourself with positive influences enhance happiness. This mindset helps you see life as a journey, impacting your overall well-being. A quote that sticks with me today says:

"Never regret a day in your life. Good days give you happiness and bad days give you experience."

This quote can remind us that both happiness and adversity are essential parts of our journey. Good days fill our hearts with joy and remind us of the beauty in the world, while bad days teach us resilience, strength, and wisdom.

Afterword

Overcome and Surpass: Rising Beyond Limits to Create Your Own Path

"Never let anyone define who you should be or what you should do. The world's opinions are not your truth—trust your instincts. Others may try to place their limits on you, but remember, you are limitless until you accept those limits as your own." – Kristi Maggio

If you are reading this, then you have made it through all these incredible examples of what positive change can create and what you as a young person can do to make your mark on this world. We are here to inspire and uplift those around us. We are here for a purpose. We each have a unique purpose that God has given us, and it is up to us to make sure that we use that purpose for the greater good. You cannot and will never be content following what someone else wants you to do, and it is hard to listen to your voice when the world can be so loud.

Over the past two years, my journey has evolved in ways I never imagined. My purpose was first to overcome challenges in my life, and in doing so, to show others how they can overcome theirs. When the way isn't clear to me, I trust that God has a way. But overcoming is just the beginning. Now, I must surpass what I've done—to reach more people, help more youth, transform education, and provide access to the resources that teach success and make it sustainable.

In *Young Changemakers Volume 2*, I've chosen to go beyond simply overcoming. Now, I'm here to surpass, to set my sights higher than I ever have because I know I can and I know I will. It took me over 40 years to fully understand this, but that's why I'm here—to share it with you so that you may learn it sooner.

I know you'll have your own challenges, make your own mistakes, and carve your own path. My hope is that this book, and the inspiration you find in these young changemakers, can make it a little easier to overcome what you face. Remember that life is a journey with twists, turns, detours, and pit stops— these aren't setbacks, but powerful parts of everyone's journey. They make you stronger, more resilient, and build perseverance.

Life isn't just about getting past obstacles; it's about moving beyond what we thought possible. Surpassing is about becoming more than we believed we could be. So, remember:

Limits Are Often Illusions
The world will tell you that certain things are "impossible" or "not for you," but remember: those limits are theirs, not yours. Challenge those boundaries and push through. You are capable of more than they'll ever understand, and only you get to decide what's possible.

Your Inner Strength Is Greater Than You Know
Every obstacle can seem overwhelming, but strength grows in response to challenges. When you face setbacks, look within. That resilience inside you is like a muscle—the more you use it, the stronger it gets.

Dream Beyond What's Expected
You might feel pressure to fit into a mold, to play it safe, or to aim for what's "realistic." But surpassing means dreaming big, reaching further, and redefining what's "realistic." Hold onto your vision, and don't settle for someone else's idea of success.

Failure Is Not Final; It's a Steppingstone
When things don't go your way, don't see it as a stop sign. Instead, view each failure as a steppingstone. Every setback teaches you something new, preparing you for an even

greater comeback. Success doesn't come from avoiding failure; it comes from surpassing it.

Believe in Your Unique Path

It's easy to compare yourself to others and feel like you're falling behind. But your journey is your own, and no one else's timeline applies to you. Surpassing means focusing on your path and finding purpose in every step.

Others' Doubts Do Not Define You

People may doubt you, question your dreams, or try to hold you back. Remember, their doubts are about *their* limitations, not yours. Don't let anyone else's fears dictate what you can achieve. Surpass those doubts, and let your actions speak louder than their words.

Find Strength in Every Obstacle

Every obstacle you encounter is a chance to go further than you thought possible. It might feel like a setback, but it's really a setup for something greater. Surpassing means using those challenges to grow, to learn, and to discover strengths you didn't know you had.

Stay Focused on What You're Capable Of, Not on What Could Go Wrong

Fear will try to keep you from taking risks. When you're faced with the unknown, remind yourself of your ability to adapt, to overcome, and to grow. Focus on what you can do, not on what might go wrong. Surpass your fears by trusting your potential.

Pave Your Own Path

It's easy to think you have to follow a certain path, but surpassing means creating one that is uniquely yours. Let your heart lead you, and don't be afraid to go in a direction that's different. Greatness often lies off the beaten path.

You Are Always Capable of More Than You Think
In moments of doubt, remind yourself that there's more inside you waiting to be unlocked. Surpassing is about pushing those boundaries, proving to yourself that you can always go further than you ever imagined. Trust in your ability to continually grow, and never stop reaching.

This chapter of your life is about going beyond what you once thought possible. Surpassing means defying limits, challenging old beliefs, and reaching heights you didn't know you could. It's about proving to yourself, again and again, that you are capable of more than you realized. This journey is about strength, resilience, and courage. By embracing the mindset to surpass, you set yourself up to not only reach your goals but to redefine them, leaving a legacy of growth and greatness for those who will follow.

If I could go back and talk to my younger self, I would tell her to *surpass* every limit and expectation—especially the ones set by others. I would remind her that every obstacle, every "no," and every doubt was not a reason to stop but an invitation to rise higher.

AUTHOR BIOS

THE TIME IS NOW TO MAKE YOUR MARK.

#ENERGY

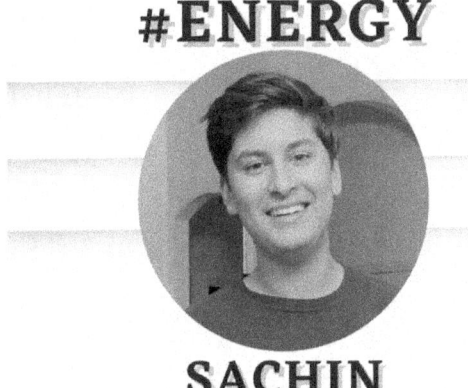

SACHIN

UNITED STATES

Sachin Syal is a 17-year-old award-winning entrepreneur and podcaster based in the Silicon Valley. As the host of The O'ChakDe Show, the first revenue-generating business and self-improvement podcast for teens, hosted by a teen, Sachin interviews influential entrepreneurs, executives, and investors encouraging young people to "go for it!" and chase their dreams. He is also the co-founder & CEO of 3Doshas, a wellness and lifestyle coaching platform that integrates Yoga & Ayurveda to help people level up and reach their full potential.

Learn more about Sachin:

https://www.youtube.com/ochakde

https://www.ochakde.com/

https://www.3doshas.com/

THE TIME IS NOW TO MAKE YOUR MARK.

#PASSION

AMEER

Jordan

Ameer El-Kurd, 16, is a tech innovator and creator of *Pleasidea*, a platform aimed at solving global challenges through technology. He is passionate about designing AI systems that support mental health and developing robots to perform labor-intensive tasks. Ameer's work reflects his belief in the power of technology to improve lives and build a better future for all.

Connect with Ameer:

https://www.linkedin.com/in/ameer-elkurd-ba05bb267/

THE TIME IS NOW TO MAKE YOUR MARK.

#CONNECT

BIAH

Pakistan

Biah Umer Khan is an A-level student from Lahore, Pakistan. She is very passionate about journalism and community service and has been able to combine both these interests through her NGO Irteqaa. A project very dear to her is Irteqaa's child education task force which she co-founded last year. In her free time, she enjoys reading, writing, and although she hates to admit it, scrolling through Instagram reels.

Connect with Biah:

Linkedin.com/in/biah-umer-khan-6042b0316

THE TIME IS NOW TO MAKE YOUR MARK.

#FAITH

JADON

United States

Jadon Lemmonds is an 18-year-old student-athlete and aspiring entrepreneur from the United States, driven by a passion for financial literacy, hands-on learning, and life skills. With a strong commitment to social impact, leadership development, and community service, Jadon actively seeks to make a difference both on and off the field.

Connect with Jadon:

https://www.instagram.com/jadonlemmonds/

THE TIME IS NOW TO MAKE YOUR MARK.

#GROWTH

SHRUSTI

India

Shrusti Mhetre, 19, is a young entrepreneur and advocate for financial independence based in India. Shrusti is focused on helping students acquire the skills necessary to earn money and achieve their goals. She actively supports environmental initiatives like *SaveSoil* and is passionate about sharing knowledge through conferences to empower young people to succeed.

Connect with Shrusti:

https://www.instagram.com/affiliate_shrusti

THE TIME IS NOW TO MAKE YOUR MARK.

KHUSHI

United States

Khushi Shah, 19, is a tech innovator, entrepreneur, and founder/CEO of Drizzl - a smart irrigation system that addresses water conservation issues. A global youth mentor, media personality, and Northeastern University student, Khushi's greater mission is to inspire other young innovators to jump out of their comfort zones and create solutions that have real-world impact.

Learn more about Khushi:

https://khushishah.org/
www.linkedin.com/in/khushishah-ceo

THE TIME IS NOW TO MAKE YOUR MARK.

#PEACE

VASUNDHARA

India

Vasundhara Chaudhary, 19, is a mental health advocate from India dedicated to breaking the stigma surrounding mental health. She founded *Inspire Dose*, a youth organization that raises awareness through social media, podcasts, and counseling initiatives. Vasundhara is passionate about creating safe spaces for people to care for their mental health just as they do their physical health.

Learn more about Vasundhara:

https://inspiredoseindia.wixsite.com/website

THE TIME IS NOW TO MAKE YOUR MARK.

#COMPASSION

SARAH

Pakistan

Sarah Sami, 14, is a health advocate and visual communicator from Pakistan who is deeply involved in raising awareness about underrepresented health issues in her country. Through her work in digital design and community service, Sarah aims to inspire empathy, promote cultural understanding, and make a lasting impact on her community and beyond.

Connect with Sarah:

https://www.linkedin.com/in/sarah-sami-0610a0318/

THE TIME IS NOW TO MAKE YOUR MARK.

#RESILIENCE

TANUJ

India

Tanuj Samaddar, 19, is an artist, social activist, and youth advocate from India. He uses his art to address contemporary social issues and is a champion for mental health awareness through his role as a peer counselor, where his creativity and resilience drive his mission to inspire a generation based on moral strength and empathy. Tanuj is a fellow of the Royal Society of Arts, a two-time presidential award-winning artist and the recipient of the Karmaveer Chakra Award from the United Nations. His role as a Councilor in the Global Youth Advisory Council - Zimbabwe is noteworthy where he has launched multiple projects including YOUTHCONNECT and ART4SERENITY to address mental health issues faced by youth. He is also an international children's peace prize nominee for 2022.

Connect with Tanuj:
https://www.linkedin.com/in/tanuj-samaddar-frsa-225020208/

THE TIME IS NOW TO MAKE YOUR MARK.

KEVIN

Canada

Kevin Kyle Keanu Shephard, 16, is a Canadian entrepreneur and content creator specializing in e-commerce and drop-shipping. His goal is to inspire young people to achieve financial freedom by teaching them the skills they need to succeed from anywhere in the world. Kevin believes that confidence and perseverance are key to unlocking success.

THE TIME IS NOW TO MAKE YOUR MARK.

#IMAGINE

MEHRISH

Pakistan

Mehrish Ali Bukhari, 16, is a writer, artist, and aspiring doctor from Pakistan who believes that imagination is key to solving the world's greatest challenges. Mehrish is committed to using her creativity to make a difference in healthcare, with a particular focus on building hospitals in rural areas of Pakistan to improve access to quality care.

Learn more about Mehrish:

http://www.beingmehrish.com

THE TIME IS NOW TO MAKE YOUR MARK.

#COBRA

SEAN KANAN

Photo Credit: Raquel Krelle Photography

Sean Kanan is an Emmy award winning producer, Emmy nominated actor, best-selling author, and motivational speaker known for his dynamic career in film and television, as well as his impactful work as an advocate for personal growth and transformation. Best known for his roles in popular shows like *The Bold and the Beautiful*, *General Hospital*, and *Cobra Kai*, Sean has built a reputation for portraying characters with depth and intensity. Beyond acting, Sean is the best-selling author of *Way of the COBRA*, a motivational book that encourages readers to embrace their inner strength and live with authenticity. He has also published *Welcome to the Kumite* the sequel to *Way of the COBRA* and *Way of the COBRA Couples edition*. Through his writing and speaking engagements, Sean inspires others to overcome obstacles, build character, and pursue meaningful success.

Learn more about Sean:

https://wayofthecobra.com/

THE TIME IS NOW TO MAKE YOUR MARK.

#INTUITION

QUEENIE DONALDSON

Queenie Donaldson is an entrepreneur, talent executive, and CEO of Queens Entertainment Group, Inc., a company that specializes in talent management, event production, and media consulting. With a career spanning over two decades in the entertainment industry, Queenie has worked with some of the biggest names in music, television, and film, helping to shape the careers of top talent and produce high-impact events. Known for her leadership, creativity, and business acumen, Queenie is passionate about empowering others to follow their dreams and embrace personal growth. She is committed to helping others unlock their potential and build fulfilling careers and lives.

Learn more about Queenie:

https://queensentertainmentgroup.com/

THE TIME IS NOW TO MAKE YOUR MARK.

#UNCOMMON

LAUREN LAPOINTE

Lauren LaPointe is a serial entrepreneur, philanthropist, and business consultant who empowers entrepreneurs and creatives to achieve their goals and build thriving, purpose-driven businesses. With a background in corporate leadership and a passion for the arts, Lauren combines practical business strategies with heart-centered guidance, helping clients around the world unlock their potential and transform their visions into reality. Through her coaching programs, workshops, and online courses, she teaches individuals how to align their passions with sustainable business practices. Lauren's mission is to inspire others to pursue their dreams while creating meaningful and impactful work.

Learn more about Lauren:

https://laurenlapointe.com/

THE TIME IS NOW TO MAKE YOUR MARK.

#IMPACT

JONA LEMMONDS

Jona Lemmonds is a business investor, keynote speaker, managing consultant, entrepreneur and a mom of six. She is the founder of The JSL Group, a consulting global venture partner and Launch Your Wealth, a platform dedicated to educational content focused on wealth creation, professional development, and principles of designing success in life. Jona actively talks and shares about the ideas of wealth, and the possibilities around it, with over 20 years + of experience in business, real estate and finance. Her mission is to inspire, represent, and elevate the wealth movement around the world.

Learn more about Jona:

https://launchyourwealth.com/

THE TIME IS NOW TO MAKE YOUR MARK.

#SURPASS

KRISTI MAGGIO

Kristi Maggio is an "EDUpreneur" working to create, shape, and impact the next generation of success stories. With over 20 years of experience in the education industry, Kristi has witnessed many children struggle and feel inadequate due to not fitting into the traditional ways of learning. When she realized she couldn't make significant change from within the system, she started creating her own. Determined to make a difference, she founded Maggio Multicultural Academy in 2016, which has since been awarded US accreditation through Cognia. Now any student from anywhere in the world can study through the academy to receive a US high school diploma. Her mission is to impact the lives of 1 billion youth in the next 10 years, create satellite locations around the world, and develop an educational program based on entrepreneurship and applied learning.

Learn more about Kristi:

https://kristimaggio.com/